Prayers of
*New Hope*

# Prayers of
# *New Hope*

Maria Aiello

# Prayers of *New Hope*

Copyright ©2020 Maria Aiello. All rights reserved.

No part of this book may be reproduced without written permission, except in the case of brief quotations in critical articles and reviews. For more information, contact admin@inscribepress.com.

Unless otherwis noted, Bible quotations are from the New King James Version®. Copyright © 1982 by Thomas Nelson. Used by permission. All rights reserved.

Verses marked NIV taken from the Holy Bible, New International Reader's Version®, NIrV® Copyright © 1995, 1996, 1998, 2014 by Biblica, Inc.™ Used by permission of Zondervan. www.zondervan.com The "NIrV" and "New International Reader's Version" are trademarks registered in the United States Patent and Trademark Office by Biblica, Inc.™

Verses marked NLT taken from the Holy Bible, New Living Translation, copyright ©1996, 2004, 2015 by Tyndale House Foundation. Used by permission of Tyndale House Publishers, a Division of Tyndale House Ministries, Carol Stream, Illinois 60188. All rights reserved.

Verses marked MSG taken from *THE MESSAGE*, copyright © 1993, 2002, 2018 by Eugene H. Peterson. Used by permission of NavPress. All rights reserved. Represented by Tyndale House Publishers, a Division of Tyndale House Ministries.

Verses marked RSV taken from the Revised Standard Version of the Bible, copyright © 1946, 1952, and 1971 National Council of the Churches of Christ in the United States of America. Used by permission. All rights reserved worldwide.

Versed mareked TPT taken from The Passion Translation®. Copyright © 2017, 2018 by Passion & Fire Ministries, Inc. Used by permission. All rights reserved. ThePassionTranslation.com.

Published by Inscribe Press, Fredericksburg, VA
ISBN 978-1-7327707-5-1 (print)
    978-1-951611-08-8 (e-book)

## **DEDICATION:**

I dedicate this book of prayers to New Hope Church in Clarion, Pennsylvania. I am especially grateful for pastors that acknowledge the gifts of the Spirit and provide a place and a way for the body to share what God has placed within them. New Hope Church has a heart to bring heaven down to earth; what a special place to worship, learn, and pray together. I have been blessed beyond words at this special place that welcomes the Holy Spirit every time we gather. Pastors Colin and Dawn Koch—long may you run.

# CONTENTS

| | |
|---|---|
| **Preface** | ix |
| **Introduction** | xi |

## Prayers of the Deep
| | |
|---|---|
| Rivers of Deep Waters | 3 |
| Dreams | 6 |
| More | 8 |
| Living Deep | 16 |

## Prayers of Light
| | |
|---|---|
| Rescue | 27 |
| Restart: Success | 33 |
| God's Staff | 41 |
| Reward | 47 |

## Prayers of Life
| | |
|---|---|
| Wrecked | 57 |
| No Graves | 66 |
| I am Who God Says I Am | 72 |

## Prayers of Triumph
| | |
|---|---|
| Heaven Steps | 81 |
| Winning At Life | 84 |
| What Satan Doesn't Want You to Know | 90 |

## Prayers of Goodness and Glory
| | |
|---|---|
| Elect Goodness | 99 |
| The Greatest Name | 103 |
| Focus | 105 |
| Glory | 111 |
| Everlasting Hope | 115 |

## Prayers of Treasure
Riches 121
Breakthrough 127
Tailspin 135

## Prayers that Make a Way
The Door 141

## Acknowledgments 147

## About the Author 149

# **PREFACE**

This work was not originally meant for publication, but for sharing orally during corporate prayer time each Sunday morning. However, God began to show me that I was meant to take my notes and form a book. So, as you read, keep in mind its original form and purpose, which was to reflect on what we were learning corporately and apply it to our prayer lives.

The book is divided into themes. These are the "titles" you see throughout, followed by a short series of thoughts and prayers, which were developed through prayer and reflection about the upcoming message title. (The series and message titles were developed by Pastor Colin Koch.)

May you be blessed by these thoughts and prayers as you read.

I urge you, the reader, to find a space, a time, and a place to talk to God. Communicate with Him using your own words, your spiritual words, and most importantly, the written Word of God. We have heard that prayer changes things. It does! So, why not press into prayer and get about changing your life, and others' lives—for your sake, for their sake, and for heaven's sake.

> Romans 15:13 (NIV): May the God of HOPE fill you with all joy and peace as you trust in Him, so that you may overflow with HOPE by the power of the Holy Spirit.

# INTRODUCTION

## HOW SHALL WE APPROACH PRAYER?

When asked to serve as the prayer minister at my home church, I was encouraged to share with the congregation what God placed upon my heart regarding what prayer should "be" within our body. Holy Spirit said loud and clear that it was to be centered around the Truth—the Word of God—and around knowing the Father's heart.

> Zephaniah 3:15: The Lord has taken away your punishment, He has turned back your enemy. The Lord, the King of Israel is with you; never again will you fear any harm. (NIV)

Let this truth sink into your soul to push out any concepts or lies you have believed that are not from God. Our perceptions, our hurts, our selfish desires (even the so-called righteous ones) can cause us to approach prayer in dishonesty. This is hardly ever intentional, but it is fleshly.

Our souls can help or hinder us in our prayers. That is why we must look to Scripture to guide us through our prayers. Hebrews 4:12 (NIV) tells us:

> For the Word of God is alive and active. Sharper than any double-edged sword, it penetrates even to dividing soul and spirit, joints and marrow; it judges the thoughts and attitudes of the heart.

So, praying the Word is praying truth. When we pray the Scriptures, we pray from a Godly place and perspective. A holy perspective. Doing this removes our intentions and tendency to pray a specific outcome. The Word is our helper. When we pray truth, we are praying effective prayers that "availeth much" (James 5:16). God is calling His bride to spend time in the Word. He is urging us because He wants to bring about His will now. He longs for us to partner in this. Are we good partners? Are we trying to make things happen, or are we cooperating with God and allowing Him to work through us?

Our working for God, for the Kingdom, begins with prayer. Prayer happens all day and everywhere as long as we keep the line of communication open; but earth-shattering prayers that change circumstances happen in the secret place with Him. In the secret place, He calls to us and whispers what he has purposed within us. It's in the secret place that the Father's heart is revealed to us, through truth and the secrets He reveals. God is waiting for us to meet Him more often in the secret place, the place where we sit at His feet.

Jeremiah 33:3:

> "Call to me and I will answer you, and show you great and mighty things, which you do not know." (NIV)

> This is God's message; communication from the God who made the earth, made it livable and lasting, the being known everywhere as God: "Call to me and I will answer you. I'll tell you marvelous and wondrous things that you could never figure out on your own." (MSG)

So, what God is saying is, "Remember the times I have given you a word or brought Scripture to your lips at the exact moment it was needed, and it caused a change or shift? Well, that is what I want to do more and more, but I'm asking for your attention, your ear, your heart, and your time. Endeavor with me in this: that the Truth will always be written on your lips, the Truth that was from the beginning (John 1:1) and the truths of my heart that you searched out as treasure in the quiet, secret place."

So, believe Zephaniah 3:15. Let it push back any darkness in your life, allowing the light of truth to shine forth. God is always faithful to reveal the Truth to us when we ask. Let us, in every situation, ask for truth. Truth is foundational to all we do, all we say, and that in which we hope.

# 1

# Prayers of
# *the Deep*

# RIVERS OF DEEP WATERS

## GOD'S HEART: TRAVAILING PRAYERS

My pastor recently shared with our church that if we haven't cried over something lately, we haven't cared enough. This is a true statement.

Travailing prayer is making a way for the heart of God to grieve through us. Simply, God speaks to us about what grieves His heart. Travailing prayers are a result of nurturing the promise for a particular person or situation. This promise speaks of God's will. When one decides to carry the truth around in their heart, they are encouraging God's will to become evident through their earnest prayer and honest belief that God is going to move on behalf of this person or situation. God sees the person or situation's future; He knows the end result if we pray—and if we don't. When it is time for something to be "birthed" spiritually God is looking for a way to be opened. Our tears, our prayers, and our cries unto God cause pressure. As we pour out to Him what He placed within us our hope erupts and His love responds. This opens a way, just like a dam breaking. We make a "way" for the prayer to be manifested on the earth by connecting with God's heart and its utterances.

When we experience these deep encounters with the heart of God, it undergirds and more clearly reveals what we have already been feeling about the person or situation we are praying for. Psalm 42:7 speaks about deep calling out to deep, and nothing is deeper than the heart of God. When our inner man meets with its Creator, we could say deep cries out to deep. This is the place where travailing prayer is created and expressed, usually through tears. Travailing prayer is a literal crying out to God from your core, asking Him to bring about change that you know only He can accomplish through the completed work on the Cross; and in that crying out, you express your willingness to carry the burden with Him until the tide is turned. Be encouraged when God calls you to the deep place on someone's behalf, because Matthew 11:30 tells us,

> "For my yoke is easy to bear, and the burden I give you is light." (NLT)

## ARE YOU PRAYING FROM THE PIT OR FROM THE WELL?

Often, we face situations in our lives that cause us to feel or believe that satan is digging a hole for us to fall into; but God, in His sovereignty, tells us that He is creating a well.

He is telling us to lift up our eyes and pray in faith from the well. Even in a deep well, we are surrounded by living water. We are full of living water in that place, for the Spirit of God is within us. This water is a powerful current that moves us. It is an endless fountain, a refreshing cascade that causes obstacles to be removed and washes over our hearts and minds, making them clear.

Revelation 22:1 reveals the astonishing picture of the river of the water of life, clear as crystal, flowing from the throne of God. In John 4:10, we read the story of Jesus meeting a Samarian woman at Jacob's well in the town of Sychar. Jesus initiates conversation with her, and informs the woman that if she knew the gift of God, and understood who was speaking to her, she would ask Him for living water. In our day, we too must become a people that understands the gift of God. So, let's pray together from the well! Let us pour out the well of life within us. Let us place the difficult situations we are contending for at His feet and begin to pray from the well, allowing Holy Spirit to draw us out of the pit as we believe for the impossible.

*Lord, forgive us for forgetting the glorious privilege of our inheritance, and praying from the pit too often. We come to you and we give you our impossibilities. We do this as we take a stand in the living waters—the well that is full of your provision and love. We believe you are responding to our willingness to pray from the wellspring of life. In your response, and in your divine answers, we will see your truth in our circumstances become crystal clear. Thank you, Lord, for washing and cleansing us and making all things new, and for the goodness growing up from the waters.*

*2 Corinthians 5:17: Therefore if any man be in Christ, he is a new creature: old things are passed away; behold, all things are become new. (KJV)*

# DREAMS

## TIMELY PRAYERS

All time belongs to God—even our sleep or "dream" time. Our prayers can enrich our dreams and our dreams our prayers.

Let's marry our dream lives with our prayer lives. I am using the term "dreams" broadly. These may be daydreams, God-given heart's desires, or our dreams at night while we sleep. Let one pour into the other, enriching them all. Our God is so big. He is a wonder; truly too big and majestic for us to fully comprehend even when using all our faculties. He knows this, so He graciously gives us ways to understand Him more fully. Sometimes dreams are the avenue He chooses. I say "avenue," because if we have a God-given dream it is meant to take us somewhere!

God is calling us to dream with Him. When you talk to Him about your dreams you are praying. Prayers aren't always about petitions and to-do lists, but about true dreaming with the Creator. We find instances of this in Scripture. In prison, Joseph learned that his cellmates were sad because they could find no one to interpret their important dreams. Joseph replied,

> "…do not the meaning or interpretation of our dreams belong to God?" (Genesis 40:8)

God talked to Gideon in the night (Judges Chapter 7) and told him to go into the enemy's camp and listen to what the men were saying. When Gideon arrived, the men were speaking about a dream. Knowledge of this dream gave Gideon enough faith to do what God was telling him to do. God wants to expand our prayer lives so we will come to Him with a posture of confidence; He desires that we would have enough confidence to ask for dreams, listen to our God-given dreams, and act upon the message found there if He bids us.

*Oh, God, Giver of dreams, expand our minds and hearts to accept what you are telling us. May we leave the interpretation to you, and as we dream let it be your creative worth that comes forth. May we be steadfast and hold tight to what it is you are calling us to. May our dreams bring us closer to our true selves and to you, our divine Creator. May we be a people who dream with you, believe you, and discern the times with you. Thank you that you continually want to commune and converse with us, even when we sleep.*

*Awaken in us the desire to dream and to understand. Let us be like Solomon and ask for wisdom. (1 Kings 3:7-9) May we find it within your Word and within our dreams.*

# MORE

## FULLNESS OF GOD, FULLNESS OF LIFE

John 10:10 NIV: "I have come that they may have life; and have it to the full."

This is the abundant life. If we are to be full and lacking nothing, we must hunger for God and make room for Him. How shall we pray to make this happen?

God is calling us to feast upon Him and His goodness, leaving no room for worldly distractions. Nothing can satisfy us like the goodness of God.

Recently, I attended a conference and heard about an account that happened in Korea. The speaker had visited the country to minister to the people. During one of the sessions she said she spoke about the Lord for forty-five minutes and the entire time she spoke the crowd that was gathered was so hungry for the Truth that they stood leaning in towards her, intent to take in all that she had to share. She continued to tell us how easy it was for the crowd to receive a miracle because of their hunger and the atmosphere that it created. The speaker went on to say that many miracles took place that night because the people were so very hungry for God. They were genuine in their pursuit of Him. When we want Jesus more than anything else, we tend to receive Him and all His benefits. (Psalm 103:2) This group of believers put themselves in a position (literally) to accept all God had for them.

Let us pray that we would be hungry and partake with the Lord and let Him fill us up.

*Lord, may we sup with you. Partake with you. Before we come to your banquet table, empty what isn't meant to be in us. Empty us of ourselves so you can be added, and may every ingredient be poured into us that we are lacking. Some of us need a dash of temperance, a pinch of gentleness, or a bushel of love. Others may need a heaping spoonful of joy. Whatever we are lacking; it is on the menu. You are sure to provide. If we need to marinate in your Word, may we take the time to do so that your flavor would come forth. May we be full and satisfied in you. May others see this in our midst and join us at the table. In Jesus' name. Amen.*

## EXPLOSIVE PRAYERS

Today we are going to pray for more faith. God is saying, "I am the Giver of gifts: the gift of faith. I have talked to you about gifts or promises that I have written on your heart; you should be expectant to receive these gifts. I have other gifts for you as well, but you do not know what they are yet. In order to obtain the gifts, you need to "set off" the gifts by lighting the fuse of FAITH!

The fireworks we love to see in the night sky are all fairly similar before they are ignited. Some may be bigger than others, or come in a slightly different package, but they are comparable in appearance and generally consistent. However, once the fuse is ignited, they explode and show the differences contained within. The amazing surprises of color and the intricate shapes and patterns become clear.

The anatomy of a firework consists of a paper or plastic outer shell that holds everything together. Inside the shell is gunpowder which is embedded with explosives called "stars." The stars are the points of light we see when the firework explodes. The stars are coated with various metals, bringing forth different colors depending on the overlying metal. As the star burns, two fuses are lit simultaneously. The first fuse that ignites is what causes the firework to be propelled into the air. The second fuse, called the "time delay" fuse, ignites a few seconds later once it reaches a certain altitude.[1]

Within the anatomy of a firework, God is giving us a creative picture of our potential, and His beauty and perfect timing. We are fireworks, because we hold the promises of God's potential. Our bodies—individually and collectively—house the Holy Spirit—God within us. The fuses are the promises, the hopes, the Godly desires, the "knowing" that there is *more*. The stars are the manifestations of the promises coming to fruition at just the right time and place. And, our *faith* is the flame, the fire that produces ignition to lift us into heavenly realms.

Let's pray for more faith.

*Isaiah 40:26 (NASB) "Lift up your eyes on high and see who created the stars, the one who leads forth their host by number, He calls them all by name; because of the greatness of His might and strength of His power, not one of them is missing."*

*Oh Lord, in the greatness of your might and strength of your power, we can believe that each promise (star) that you have placed within us will explode and make a show of your great might as we let faith arise in us. You are the provider of our faith. Help us in our unbelief to grab hold of the promises with heavenly faith. May we begin to see the manifestation of your faithfulness in our lives, and may it begin the celebration of a life-long display of your majesty. Glory to you, Lord!*

## NOW IS THE TIME—FAMILY TIME
## GOD WANTS MORE FOR YOUR FAMILY

God invented time. He ordered it. And, He set it into motion: time ticking by. And yet, He isn't bound by it. He can speed it up or slow it down. He can stop it. He can place special attributes within a period of time, such as a "*Kairos* time." *Kairos* carries with it the idea of the "right time."

God is causing prayerful people to be awakened to the notion that now is the time for family restoration. Imagine how that would ignite faith in the body of Christ. People would begin to say, "If God can do *this* in my family, I know he can do _____!" How many of God's people are weary and feel hopeless in the presence of family strife or sin because they seem to have no solutions to bring about change. But God is saying **now** is the time.

The amazing thing about God is that He has the answers. The wondrous thing about God is that He even tells us how to get the answers!

If God wants to order the family now, and you are holding out hope, let this ignite your prayer life, and energize your faith.. If you are waiting and believing, and what you prayed hasn't happened yet, don't feel foolish or discouraged because your heart's desires are right on time. God is showing up!

The Holy Spirit is speaking this Kingdom family message: "This is the time to pray for family. Pray differently. Pray what I am saying and pray how I tell you to pray. Take the lid off your box and begin to venture outside your comfortable realm of sweet or hopeful prayers. Begin to take your family back! You may be the only one willing; they need you now."

If you feel like God is asking you to do some things that don't make sense, just do them! I currently have a sock in my Bible that Holy Spirit told me to place there until a family member comes to know the Truth! I had been interceding for this person for a long time. I was waking up at night and praying, praying all day sometimes; I couldn't let the situation go. God had put it in my heart to contend for this soul that He and I love so much. I was to the point I thought I couldn't keep up the intercession much longer, until one day I found the sock and was led to put it in my Bible. Now, when I see it, I pray in faith and move on, because God asked me to do a new thing in this time. Just this simple act of obedience provided me a release and a place of peace that is founded on faith in my Father to come through for this situation. Sounds strange, but His ways are not our ways, and for that I am thankful!

So, in the meantime, in the now time, as you wait, act upon what the Holy Spirit is prodding you to do. Maybe it's a whisper you hear. Maybe it's a "sock thing" you are being led to—it could be something simple or maybe even a little scary. You might be thinking "How could that be it? You want me to do that?"

Yes, He does.

Think of your family: biological, spiritual or adopted. God has more blessings than you are aware of for the people you love, because He loves them more than you are capable of. God has opened a window in this time. Let's go to the open window with our family name and any others that we love. Stand at the window as a profession of your faith, believing the promises for these loved ones. May God's Spirit blow through the window and put your family back in order. The breath of God brings life and strength to us; strength to love well. It's also able to disperse the dirt and the old patterns of poor communication and disconnection. His breath, His life, is what every family needs.

*Lord, we stand before the open window. What shall you have us do? Shout out the window? Watch out the window? Imagine what is out there? Possibilities? Maybe you want us to reach out and pull more of you down, or pull someone in.*

*As we set our eyes on you, looking out the window, may we "decree a thing and it will be established for (us) and a light will shine on (our) ways." (Job 22:28) Oh, God you "hath made (our) mouths like a sharp sword, in the shadow of (your) hand hath (you) hid us; and made us a polished shaft; in (your) quiver hath (you) hid us." (Isaiah 49:2). May our words be your words: words of truth, words of love, words straight from heaven that gather our families. In Jesus' name, amen.*

## MULTIPLICATION—TAKE WHAT YOU HAVE TO THE FATHER IN PRAYER

God is multiplying what we have—what He has given us already.

He is multiplying our resources; naturally and spiritually. God wants us to understand what He has given us and then we are to learn to steward it well; this is known as multiplication. God doesn't waste anything, ever. He understands supply and demand better than anyone, and His supply is unending. He is the infinite resource.

So, imagine when you pray and ask for *more*, you already have what you need. Think about Moses. He already had the staff in his hand (Exodus chapter 4).

Moses had his staff, but he needed more. He wanted to prove that he had been with the Lord. Moses wanted to bring God into Israel's situation so the people would believe. He needed to complete the mission and to carry out the work. Moses desperately wanted to show the men that God was strong in their midst. He was determined to show the people God had more for them. Moses needed to convince the crowd of Israelites that God had a plan. When Moses and Aaron met with the elders, God used Moses' faith and the miraculous signs to multiply the Israelites faith. God did this by using what Moses already had acquired-his faith, which was developed out of time with God and the staff he had in his hand.

Remember the widow with only a little bit of oil? (2 Kings chapter 4).

The widow had a little provision, but she needed more. She was trying to save her household, and when she spoke to Elisha about her need, he told her and her sons to gather jars and go home, and behind closed doors pour what oil they did possess into the containers.

When you are in need, there is one thing necessary: you must go to Him with what you have—maybe even with what you already have in your hand or in your house. Then God can show you "the more" you already possess in Him.

Let's take what we have to the Lord.

*God, you are our provider. Show us what you want us to do with what we have; with the gifts you have already bestowed upon us. May we be good stewards of what we have and not miss the full purpose of all that you have put in our lives. Help us see what is before us, around us, and among us. Let us see and experience your provision in a fresh way. Lord, if you are asking us to share your glory with others to complete your kingdom work, like Moses, help us experience your power and have a greater revelation of what you are doing—and what you are able to do—with who you created us to be and with what you have already given us. Let others see your glory working in our lives.*

*Lord we believe you want to multiply our resources. Give us eyes to see the process. We want to see the creative strategy to bring about more of what you have for us through the current gifts we have in our homes and in our hands. May these gifts be used to the fullest measure, and in doing so, may we bring you glory. As we pray this prayer we remember Abraham, a man who already had the seed, which you multiplied into the nation of Israel. In Jesus' name we pray. Amen.*

# LIVING DEEP

## PRAYERS THAT LAST

We have talked about eternal prayers. What is deeper than eternity? It has no end, and neither do the depths of our God. Are your prayers reaching the depths? Would you say your prayers are deep, or are they shallow? Shallow prayers only see, and so only speak to, what is on the surface. This may sustain you for a while, but the longer you know God, the more you want of Him. You want to go deeper. Shallow prayers may get you through the day, but deep prayers can see you through the night. And we are all guaranteed a night season. Luke 5: 1-11 tells the events of Simon Peter and his crew fishing all night with no success. Jesus, in the morning, tells Simon to let out his nets into the deep for a catch.

> So it was, as the multitude pressed about Him to hear the word of God, that He stood by the Lake of Gennesaret, and saw two boats standing by the lake; but the fishermen had gone from them and were washing their nets. Then He got into one of the boats, which was Simon's, and asked him to put out a little from the land. And He sat down and taught the multitudes from the boat. When He had stopped speaking, He said to Simon, "Launch out into the deep and let down your nets for a catch."
>
> But Simon answered and said to Him, "Master, we have toiled all night and caught nothing; nevertheless at Your word I will let down the net." And when they had done this, they caught a great number of fish, and their net was breaking. So they signaled to their partners in the other boat to come and help them. And they came and filled both the boats, so that they began to sink. When Simon Peter saw it, he fell down at Jesus' knees, saying, "Depart from me, for I am a sinful man, O Lord!"
>
> For he and all who were with him were astonished at the catch of fish which they had taken; and so

also were James and John, the sons of Zebedee, who were partners with Simon. And Jesus said to Simon, "Do not be afraid. From now on you will catch men." So when they had brought their boats to land, they forsook all and followed Him (NKJV).

After reading this passage we see that the crew caught so many fish that they and the boats were sinking. Verse 9 says they were astonished at the catch. Their current—shall we say shallow—lives couldn't hold all that Jesus had for them. Jesus told them not to fear, because now they would catch men. Simon and his crew forsook everything in their current lives and followed Him. So, imagine if you cast your net of prayer into the deep, how much *your* life will take on. Your life, like the boat, will begin to be drawn into the depths.

*Lord, when Simon Peter and his crew were fishing they missed what was in the depths. They thought there wasn't even one fish to catch, let alone a multitude; enough to change the course of their very lives. Show us how to cast our net into the deep, having faith to pray prayers that draw out all the treasures and supply that you have waiting in the deep.*

*Oh, may we have great faith and revelation to take our prayers and supplications, place them in the net, and cast them into the deep. May we do this according to your guiding just as you led the fisherman, and then we will see there is an answer to these prayers. I decree that there are many answers, even more than our nets can hold. This day, may we be a people that draw out the goodness, the unseen treasures of the deep with prayers that go beyond the surface of what we see and know. In Jesus' name we pray and cast our nets. Amen.*

## PEACE BE STILL

Our prayers usher us into the presence of God. When we commune with the Holy Spirit in our prayer times, we draw out the deep things of God. We draw out the Living Water through stillness. Have you ever just sat in the Lord's presence, waiting to hear a word from the very voice and lips of God? If so, you know there is a stillness that is required. In the stillness we listen. Every word from God carries a revelation, and the Holy Spirit is our interpreter.

Jesus is our access to the presence of the Father. Hebrews 10:19 22 (NIV) speaks of Jesus as the Holy of Holies:

> Therefore, brothers and sisters, since we have confidence to enter the Most Holy Place by the blood of Jesus, by a new and living way opened for us through the curtain, that is, His body, and since we have a great priest over the house of God, let us draw near to God with a sincere heart and with the full assurance that faith brings, having our hearts sprinkled to cleanse us from a guilty conscience and having our bodies washed with pure water.

And we have this wondrous prayer from Paul in Ephesians 1:17 (TPT):

> I pray that the Father of glory, the God of our Lord Jesus Christ, would impart to you the riches of the Spirit of wisdom and the Spirit of revelation to know him through your deepening intimacy with Him."

The prayers we pray in stillness are the ones that bring about a revelation of the Father's heart. And doesn't His heart hold all things? If we are looking for revelation, we are looking for a closer walk with God.

*Lord, we want to go deeper. Thank you for your Spirit of wisdom and revelation. As we search for meaning and understanding may the Holy Spirit guide us so that our minds are clear, our hearts are cleansed, and our ears are opened; in this way, we gain wisdom. We are drawing near to you behind the veil, where revelation lives. The more we learn about you and experience your presence, the more is revealed to us. You are the revelation, Lord. As we draw closer to you, deep will cry out to deep, uncovering what you have for us—the treasures you have placed for us to behold. You are saying "Please be still. Peace be still." We want to meet you behind the veil. In Jesus' name. So be it.*

## CAN YOU DIG IT?

Deep worship is a result of digging out what is under the soulish part of us. It is getting to the spirit man that knows it is the righteousness of God that we should be proclaiming, the love of God that we should be thankful for, and the goodness of the Father we should be talking about.

Our prayers can take us to the heart of worship by removing us from thoughts of ourselves so we can praise and magnify God. Deep worship means praising Him no matter what. Our worship is a choice based on our relationship with Him. Our prayers, if consistent with the Word and Truth, will move out the debris of life. This makes it possible to see our Lord clearly, through the eyes of our spirit. This is how we can truly worship Him. The clutter has to go. For us to dig deep it takes some work, but this is the true labor of, love isn't it? We must express our deepest gratitude to the one who made us. This expression bursts forth in our prayers and becomes the song we sing. Our lives each carry a unique sound. So as we dig and remove and press in, and our prayers begin to demonstrate to us and our Creator that we need to exalt Him no matter what, chains begin to break, lies begin to be revealed, healing begins to manifest; and most wonderfully, you begin to understand that to give to your Creator is better than to receive from your Creator!

So, start digging. Tell God how wonderful He is even when you don't feel like it. Let your prayers move you beyond your own experience into a deeper place of trust, where your prayers speak of His infinite goodness and provision. It is good to praise God in all circumstances, but it is better to praise Him *above* your circumstances; over your entire life.

Let's praise Him together.

*Our God, whom we love, we exalt you in our lives now, before we get to the other side. We sing about your faithfulness before the answer comes. We dance before the victory materializes. We make a joyful noise even if the times we are in feel burdened and sad. We send up a shout even when it seems you are silent in our season. We want and will to praise you no matter what. We choose to boast of our God.*

> *Ephesians 5:20 NLT: And give thanks for everything to God the Father in the name of our Lord Jesus Christ.*
>
> *1 Chronicles 16:8 (NKJV): We will give thanks to the Lord and call upon His name making known his deeds among the peoples.*
>
> *Hebrews 13:15 (KJV): Through Him then, let us continually offer up a sacrifice of praise to God, that is the fruit of lips that give thanks to His name."*

*So Lord, we decree this day that our words will be expressions of praise to you and we will feast upon the fruit of our lips that bring you glory no matter what. In Jesus' name, amen*

(Family Sunday—A celebration of New Hope families held on the fifth Sunday of the month)

## FAMILIES ARE BEING RESTORED

God is telling those in His family that He wants to heal our natural families. God is giving confirmation after confirmation about His will to restore families. This is a word that we should truly receive without reservation. This is the word we should chew on, and act on it by behaving and speaking like this word is already beginning to manifest. This includes extended family members as well. God said He is going deep—deep into our family lines—"Four generations and more."

> Proverbs 15:6a ESV: In the house of the righteous there is much treasure.

When I began to pray and meditate on what this means, God said He has been causing a righteousness to grow within His people. Righteousness can be found in our homes And those that visit our homes and those that live there will experience the righteousness of God. God continues to say that those in His family who have been rooted in love, loving God above all else and valuing Him more than their own lives and family members, are growing in righteousness. Holy Spirit even began to share with me that some of us are removing things from our lives, literally from our homes, in order to be holy and righteous. God sees all of this and He is pleased. Righteousness is building our homes and growing us closer to our Father and those we love. Be encouraged today like never before about the impending restoration of your family. This promise is for future generations as well. God is going deep. Deeper than you know.

*Lord, God we thank you for this promise. You are worthy to be praised. Lord, may this root of love grow down deep into our firm foundation, which is our love in you. Let this foundation support all the treasures within our houses and our homes. Lord, we have not because we ask not, so help us to receive this word and begin to believe and ask according to your will for our families' restoration. Let the restoration begin in us. Change us, Lord, from glory to glory that we may grow in righteousness for your names' sake. God help us to go deep with you—not just to pray for salvation for those that are lost, but to go beyond that and believe for the abundant life for those you love. We receive this word today and declare that we are living among many treasures—so many that our houses will not be able to hold them all. We put you at the center of our families because you alone, God, are worthy. We pray this in Jesus' name. Amen.*

## __ENDNOTES__

1    www.acs.org  (firework anatomy information)

# 2

# Prayers of *Light*

# RESCUE

## PRAYERS OF RESCUE

Every time we see an answered prayer, it is a rescue. I see rescue plans all around the globe. They are happening. This past week I saw many things in the news that caused me to deeply thank God for all that He is doing.

Over the past few years it is apparent that many Christians are praying earnestly for our nation, and for our world. We started to see how much we need rescued! One of the synonyms for Savior is liberator. Aren't you seeing the liberty of God springing up all around?

It is good to send up a prayer of praise when we see God's goodness unfolding around us. Here are some rescue missions that have come from heaven to earth recently. Let's thank God for these:

- Kentucky governor signed a bill stating that Bible courses would be allowed as an elective in public schools to help students better understand "contemporary society and culture."[1]
- Politicians are asking for prayer as they navigate sexual harassment allegations within the government.[2]
- Museum of the Bible opens in Washington, D.C. on November 17, 2017.
- European Christians march to keep cross visible on Pope statue after courts rule to remove it.[3]
- President Donald Trump recognizes Jerusalem as Israel's capital.[4]
- Vice President Mike Pence stated the US will grant aid to persecuted Christians in the Middle East and made this statement during a recent speech: "The United States will work hand-in-hand from this day forward with faith-based groups and private organizations to help those who

are persecuted for their faith. This is the moment, now is the time, and America will support these people in their hour of need."
- Pro-life judge Neil Gorsuch was appointed to the Supreme Court.[5]

As we see the Spirit of God being invited back into our culture, our lives the liberty of God WILL follow.

2 Corinthians 3:17 (NIV) Now the Lord is the Spirit, and where the spirit of the Lord is there is freedom.

*Lord, we hope that as we praise you and thank you for the answered prayers that we will begin to recognize and experience the freedom in Christ that is ours. And that this liberty will begin to draw us near our Messiah; making us shine brightly, revealing Him to others. Thank you for the miracles happening all around us. We thank you that you honor corporate prayers of a nation and a people that believe you will answer and heal the land (2 Chronicles 7:14).*

## LIGHT IS ALWAYS PART OF THE RESCUE MISSION

Light is usually important in any rescue effort, whether it be flashing on top of an emergency vehicle; or in the operating room, guiding the doctor's eyes; a flashlight in a dark neighborhood as we search for a lost pet; a headlamp to look for a lost coalminer; a helicopter searching for a lost hiker; or a lighthouse that signals to the sailor he has arrived home after a long journey.

As I write this, it is the Christmas season, and we see many lights all around, shining and reminding us that Jesus came to save us.[6] It makes me think of those that celebrate the season, but don't truly understand the reason. They need to be rescued. The light is there; they may have even put lights up on their home or on the tree, but they don't recognize the true Light–the Light that saves and rescues us.

Jesus is the Light of the world. He tells us this in John 8:12 (NIV):

> When Jesus spoke again to the people, He said, "I am the light of the world. Whoever follows me will never walk in darkness, but will have the light of life."

Jesus is the ultimate rescue. He is the life rescue everyone is looking for. Most of us have seen searchlights; the powerful lights that shine from the ground into the sky. I found this to be a great picture of those that are looking for the ultimate life rescue. They are looking up for the Light of the world. They are searching to find heaven and discover who lives there. They are the individuals who celebrate Christmas without realizing that Christmas celebrates God's rescue for humankind. We should pray that their search light is turned upward, that they may begin to see the Lord's rescue plan. There will come a time for evacuation from this earth, and the only way into the safety of the Father is through the Son, our Savior, and our Rescue.

Lord this is a season of light, so we ask that you would shine into the darkness. We are thankful for your rescue plan for us, and for all your creation. Help those who don't know you turn their eyes and their "search light" toward you, and may their eyes and hearts be enlightened. We are hopeful that the Light of the world will shine brightly this season into the dark places revealing your saving plan—the only rescue plan that ensures life and safety for us, now and for eternity. In Jesus' name. Amen

## THE GREATEST GIFT: OUR RESCUE

God loves us so much that He gave us the greatest gift of all time: Jesus.

Think about giving someone a gift that is a real blessing to them. Doesn't it feel amazing? This is why Christmas gifts can be so joyful to give. Now imagine how it must have felt for God to know He was sending humankind His greatest gift to meet our greatest need! Jesus fulfilled all God's promises and made available everything God's children needed through every generation. Can you imagine how it would feel to give someone a gift that satisfied their every need and every desire? It's hard to envision or capture what that would be like.

So, in this Christmas season we thank God for this gift; we thank Him with prayers of celebration. Christmas is a celebration of the most perfect gift ever bestowed to mankind. Let's read Luke 2: 8-14 (NKJV):

> Now there were in the same country shepherds living out in the fields, keeping watch over their flock by night. And behold, an angel of the Lord stood before them, and the glory of the Lord shone around them, and they were greatly afraid.
> 
> Then the angel said to them, "Do not be afraid, for behold, I bring you good tidings of great joy which will be to all people. For there is born to you this day in the city of David a Savior, who is Christ the Lord. And this will be the sign to you: You will find a Babe wrapped in swaddling cloths, lying in a manger."
> 
> And suddenly there was with the angel a multitude of the heavenly host praising God and saying: "Glory to God in the highest, And on earth peace, goodwill toward men!"

No matter how many times we read or hear those verses, it's like the first time. And that is because Jesus is the gift that keeps on giving. John 1:16 (NKJV) tells us:"And of His fullness we have all received, and grace for grace."The Message reads: "We all live off his generous bounty, gift after gift after gift."

So, let us pray a prayer of celebration to our heavenly Father for the world's best gift.

*Abba, we rejoice in the Newborn King. We sing, "Joy to the World" as we thank you for giving us your only begotten Son—the Light of the world full of grace and truth. When you provided us with the gift of Jesus you gave us everything we could ever ask for.*

*If we ask for peace—Jesus is our peace.*

*If we ask for love—Jesus is love.*

*If we ask for healing—Jesus is the healer.*

*If we ask for salvation—Jesus is the Savior.*

*If we ask for truth—Jesus is the truth.*

*If we ask for direction—Jesus is the way.*

*If we ask for a friend—Jesus is by our side, sticking closer than a brother.*

*We have received the greatest gift. We celebrate with a grateful heart and praises to the newborn King on our lips. In His wonderful name, Jesus, we pray. Amen.*

# RESTART: SUCCESS

### ONE WORD CAN GET YOU STARTED

I heard a pastor on the radio this week say that we have a God who realizes that His people need a restart, so in His wisdom He created a year. He decided that we would get a new beginning each year.

A year is one revolution around the sun. Imagine if you asked God to give you a word at the beginning of each year to ponder and have at the forefront of your prayer life. This word would represent what God was speaking to you in this time. Perhaps God would reveal His desires to you for a particular season of your life—this upcoming season.

Now imagine experiencing the *Son* (Jesus) in all seasons and times this year, through the lens of His word for you—your one word.

How many times could we orbit the Son and still not see Him in His entirety? Our prayer life is how we begin to magnify Jesus in our lives. (We all know what happens with a magnifying glass and the sun on a hot day.)

We hear words like grace, favor, salvation, restoration, trust; and the list goes on. However, do we really understand the depths of these words and their godly implications in our lives? Imagine how praying "through" a year with one of these words, or any "God-thoughts," could change you, or the people you pray for?

Let's pray the Word together.

*Matthew 24:35 (NKJV): Heaven and earth will pass away, but my words will by no means pass away.*

*Psalm 119:130 (NIV): The unfolding of your words gives light; it gives understanding to the simple.*

*Matthew 4:4: But He answered and said, It is written, Man*

*shall not live by bread alone, but by every word that proceedeth out of the mouth of God.*

*Psalm 18:30 (NIV): As for God, His way is perfect. The Lord's word is flawless; He shields all who take refuge in Him.*

*Lord, we thank you for your living Word that is active in us. God, you never change; you are the same yesterday, today, and tomorrow. Thank you that we can count on you always. We know you are changing us from glory to glory as we travel around the bright and shining Star. May we have a deeper understanding, experience a greater sense of your glory, and see who you are a little more clearly as we live and move through this year with you. Jesus, may you be our only sphere of influence this year, as we pray through the next 360-degree view of you. May we magnify your name above all other names, and let it be a revolution of the old system of life for us as we start again with you. In Jesus' name. Amen*

## IT'S ALL ABOUT PERSPECTIVE

God has created every person with a unique destiny, and the personality and gifts to step into that destiny. Do you have a vision of yourself that aligns with His? Believe it or not, agreeing with the Lord's perspective is the position from which the Scriptures teach us to pray. Are you praying from a Kingdom perspective?

Think about your present prayer life. What does it consist of? Do you talk to, or with, God? Is prayer a partnership? Is it a list of requests and hopes? Is it like having lunch with a friend? Does it consist of travailing and intercession? Are there quiet seasons, clashing and clamoring seasons? Is it even silent at times?

It is probably all these things. Let's hope that is true, because our prayer life is a vital part of our relationship with God our heavenly Father. Our prayer stance depends upon our beliefs about Jesus and our surrender to the Holy Spirit's guiding.

When you are in a battle the location or position is key to victory. This is also true in your prayer life. The position from *which* you pray is more effective than *what* you pray sometimes. Your position in prayer probably resembles what you see when you look in the mirror. Most of us assess ourselves through a combination of positive and negative personal thoughts:

"I only have a little hair loss."

"My eyes aren't too bad."

"My arms could be thinner."

"I have a nice voice, but I am terrible with people."

"I am a great mathematician, but my public speaking needs a lot of help." And on and on…

Then we take this cluttered mixture of thoughts to our prayer life:

"God I know you can give me the grace and wisdom to do a good job at work, or to take good care of my family, but I just don't know if you will heal me of _____." Or, "I trust you for the day to day, but I'm not sure about eternity. I just can't wrap my mind around that." And on and on…

I believe God is telling us to reclaim His vision of us. What does God see when He looks at us? He sees His beautiful creation; His craftsmanship. We are fearfully and wonderfully made in His image. This is not to say that we should look in the mirror and glorify ourselves, but we glorify Him. God shared with me that <u>reclaiming</u> His vision of us has to do with <u>reflection,</u> meaning to embody or represent faithfully, or show an image of.

> I Corinthians 13:12 (NLT): Now we see things imperfectly, like puzzling reflections in a mirror, but then we will see everything with perfect clarity. All that I know now is partial and incomplete, but then I will know everything completely, just as God now knows me completely.

This is exactly why we cannot pray from a position built upon our beliefs of who we think we are, but we must pray and stand on what the Father says about us, because He knows us fully at this moment. He sees us completely; we do not..

To reflect is to "throw back (heat, light, sound) without absorbing it."[7] As I studied who we are in Christ, our rightful position as heirs to the throne, in conjunction with information about reflections, I learned that when we are rightly positioned we are standing on the promises and truths of our identity in Christ, embodying Him faithfully, while we throw back, immediately, what the liar says about us without absorbing it!

*Lord you are wonderful. Help us to be on guard and stand firm in the faith—the faith that reminds us that we are standing in heavenly places with Christ Jesus. This same posture of faith speaks awareness to our inner man and shares with him that we are in Christ: redeemed, loved, forgiven, strong, bold, healed, heaven-bound. We understand that we are in a place of authority in Christ. In Luke 10, Jesus told His disciples that He saw satan fall from the sky, and He gave us, His followers, authority to overcome all the power of the enemy. May we continue to stand and proclaim this authority. We bear your image, and as we do so faithfully, may we stand in authority in Jesus' name over all the failed attempts of the enemy, our defeated foe. We can say this without wavering, because we know your words are true and you are the Faithful Witness. (Revelation 1:5). In Jesus' name. Amen.*

## TRUE SUCCESS TAKES A MIRACLE (OR TWO)

Success is something I think about every day due to my current position. Success, or some definition or concept of it, is a part of my focus each day. My colleagues and I have been given the charge to support college students in finding success, whether it be academic, personal, or financial. When you are an educator you realize we are all students of something. If we are students then we are learning, moving forward, and hopefully making attempts to become successful. And if we are hoping to be successful, truly successful, then we need a miracle.

When students come in for advice, or asking for a solution to a problem, what I want to tell them is, "You need a miracle!" This is not to say that all the issues they bring to the table are daunting and without hope. But most students I know are really looking to be who they know they were created to be. This is a process for most of us and there are miracles needed along the way. When a student says they are depressed and have no motivation to go to class—they need a miracle! When a student expresses they have no idea what major to choose and are not even sure if they should be in college—they need a miracle! When a student has passed every class with flying colors and is ready to graduate and about to look for their first "grown up" job—they need a miracle! We can point students to all kinds of resources and share strategies for success, but what they really need is a miracle: the miracle of knowing who they are and realizing *whose* they are. This is where true success is found. We all know we are not truly fulfilled until we are living the God-story we were created to live. Students at any stage of life and learning need the Source of life to be accomplished people.

Since we are students, continually learning, we are in the process of receiving a miracle. Have you thought about that? I'm not saying that strategies, skills, and hard work—whether natural or supernatural—are not important, and sometimes they *are* the miracle, but in every circumstance, the common thread is the need for a miracle for any of us to live our full potential.

When someone is successful and skilled in a given area, they are known as a "specialist." The ultimate, divine specialist is our God, the Father. He is our strategy for acquiring knowledge and wisdom. He is how we can have victory in every situation. His methods never fail.

*Lord, you are the solution and answer to every problem. Jesus, you are the Teacher. You specialize in all things above and under the sun. You are the inventor, the Creator of all things. As we go through life we learn many things. We hope to be enlightened. We hope to find success. We hope to live the abundant life. The only way for us to even define these accomplishments in our individual lives is to know you and to know what you say about us. Help us to be available to your instruction. That is when we realize the formula for success: God plus Jesus plus Holy Spirt plus revelation equals victory. (Victory is another word for success.)*

*Lord, we thank you that we are bound for triumph in you. You are the definer of our earthly and eternal success. May we look to you first for wise counsel in all our endeavors. In Jesus' name we pray. Amen.*

*Psalm 1:1-3 (MSG):*
*How well God must like you—*
    *you don't hang out at Sin Saloon,*
    *you don't slink along Dead-End Road,*
    *you don't go to Smart-Mouth College.*
*Instead you thrill to GOD's Word,*
    *you chew on Scripture day and night.*
*You're a tree replanted in Eden,*
    *bearing fresh fruit every month,*
*Never dropping a leaf, always in blossom.*

*Joshua 1:8 (NKJV): "This Book of the Law shall not depart from your mouth, but you shall meditate in it day and night, that you may observe to do according to all that is written in it. For then you will make your way prosperous, and then you will have good success."*

## SUCCESS TAKES HEART

We have heard the saying "You gotta have heart." How does that look? What does this even mean? Proverbs 23:26 tells us,

> "My son give me your heart and let your eyes delight in my ways."

We must give God our heart. That is how we know we are living an authentic, genuine life—the exciting life, the righteous life, the life that others look at and say, "They have heart. They are doing it right."

Your heart is the center, or most integral part of you. Many Christians, in this season, are feeling expectant because God's glory is increasing on the earth as Jesus' return gets closer and closer. They are in anticipation of something glorious and godly. This must mean that God is whispering to their hearts. They are hearing, seeing, and experiencing God's latter day glory around them and it resonates with the deepest part of them-their heart. Maybe you feel expectant; eager to see what God is doing and what He is going to do. If so, you need to make your heart ready. Maybe you feel like you need a heart renewal. He can do that.

Psalm 51:10 says,

> "Create in me a pure heart, O God, and renew a steadfast spirit within me."

Proverbs 23:26 tells us that when we give our heart to God our eyes will delight in His ways. This is how we become expectant for the things of God.

How do we give our hearts to God? One avenue to communion with God is prayer. I Samuel 16:17 tells us that God examines the heart. Imagine that as you pray God is evaluating your heart. When we receive a medical examination, the doctor tells us our state of health. This is what God is doing with us. Are you heart-healthy? Jeremiah 17:10 explains that God searches the heart. God is always examining us, but unless you are in conversation with Him, you don't know His findings. We wait to hear back from the doctor about our examination. We always make sure we talk to our physician after a visit. We need to do the same with our God through prayer.

Think of Noah's heart. In his day, God was examining all of mankind's hearts, and He found no one, except Noah, who did not have evil in his heart. Noah was expectant and believed what God told him He was going to do; so much that Noah spent a modern-day lifetime building the ark. Noah must have continually given his heart to God as he was preparing for the floodgates of heaven and springs of the deep to open up. Genesis 6:6-7 says God's heart was filled with pain as He examined the evil hearts of men. Once the ark was completed, God opened His heart, which contains the floodgates of the heavens and the springs of the deep. I can imagine that during the flood the heart of God and the heart of Noah were in communication most of the time. Doesn't this true account of the Great Flood make you consider that God's heart desire is always to be in relationship with you? He longs to know you heart-to-heart.

When the water receded, Noah ended up on Mount Ararat, which means "holy ground." If we are expecting to reach holy ground, we better be prepared. Let God search your heart and make you ready. Noah was convincingly successful. We might be able to say he was the most successful man in history. He listened to God, engineered the ark and saved humanity!

Let us pray.

*God, we thank you that you made a promise, a covenant that you would never flood the earth again. Thank you that you are a loving Father who chose to spare a man and his family so you could continue to be joined with your creation that you love so much. Lord, as we listen to your heart, may we hear you telling us the condition of our own, so we may respond as Noah did, trusting you and believing that you are going to do what you said you would do. We need a great flood of your heart and all it contains so we can reach the holy ground—the place you are taking us to. May we prepare and build as we wait upon you, and when the time comes may we be ready because we are behind the closed door of the ark abiding in you. In Jesus' name. Amen.*

## GOD'S STAFF

**THE INTERVIEW IS JUST THE BEGINNING OF OUR STORY**
In order to get hired, we must first go through a successful interview. In this case, the interview for becoming one of God's staff members, is saying "yes" to Jesus. But, this is only the initiation of our godly work because, the interview is just the beginning of our story. Working for God is the most fulfilling career we could imagine because God writes our life story.

Scripture talks about books and scrolls quite often. This would make us think that God likes books. He does record events, like all of time and the time to come, after all.

He also writes the story of our individual lives. God chose to speak to us through a Book filled with true stories. He could have spoken to His creation any way He wanted to, but He chose a Book.

God is the author of our lives. A question we should ask ourselves is, "Am I praying from the book God has written about my days?" David says in Psalm 139:16,

> Your eyes have seen my unformed substance, and in your book were all written the days that were ordained for me when as yet there was not one of them. (NASB)

God didn't just create our physical and spiritual bodies and then stop; He has also created a story for each of us. Our story is an integral part of our creation. God writes a beautiful story for each of us, for He is the author of our lives.

Our books are in heaven; our stories. When we find ourselves with a sense that we are made for more, we are catching a glimpse of the pages in our book. Our identity is found within Jesus, the Word of God, but I believe it is also found within the story of who

God made us; our personal gifts are part of the narration. Our God-given gifts and talents are unique to us and our individual story. They are ours to use in every area of our lives, especially within our work, our careers and our callings. Where has God called you to go? What has His story whispered to your heart? The following verse proves that God has written the book on our hearts:

In 2 Corinthians 3:3 Paul states:

> You show that you are a letter from Christ the result of our ministry, written not with ink but with the Spirit of the living God, not on tablets of stone, but on tablets of human hearts. (NIV)

> You yourselves are all the endorsement we need. Your very lives are a letter that anyone can read by just looking at you. Christ himself wrote it—not with ink, but with God's living Spirit; not chiseled into stone, but carved into human lives—and we publish it. (MSG)

When we live in a way that displays who we are—and others see Jesus in us—we are living out our heavenly biography. Let's pray that our book will become an international best-seller.

*Lord, you are the author and perfecter of our faith. We thank you that you have a story for each one of us. We praise you for your goodness and complete work in our personal creation. Thank you that you love us so deeply that you ordained all the days of our lives. Thank you that our story, all of our days, are exciting, true, righteous, and full of virtue. May we seek you and find the truth of our story. May we cherish and pursue the divine work that each of us embodies. As we pray for ourselves and others, may it be with a heart and intention of opening the book so your creation and endless good works can continue; revealing your glory. Your glory is in us. In Jesus' name. Amen.*

## THE ULTIMATE CONSULTANT

We live in a time of where many businesses and organizations hire consultants to help solve a problem, provide direction, or improve business and productivity.

A "consultant" is a person who provides expert advice professionally. God has sent us a divine Consultant. Our Father provides every opportunity for us to learn about our worth, our identity, and our gifts. This is so we can understand the message our existence should portray: one that magnifies God. Aren't we to be joyously working at knowing these truths? God is the most honorable and kind-hearted employer we could imagine. He leaves no room for us to ever have the opportunity to say, "I didn't know how to do it." We have all we need to do the best work in our natural and spiritual lives. We have the most profound help in the Holy Spirit. He is the Consultant; He is the first and the last.

We need to remember that our prayers are a direct line to the Ultimate Consultant. Jesus told us that God would send us a wise Consultant:

> I John 14:26 (RSV) "But the Counselor, the Holy Spirit, whom the Father will send in my name, He will teach you all things, and bring to your remembrance all that I have said to you."

Let's imagine what may have happened. After Jesus accomplished the greatest work in history, He returned to heaven and sat down by His Father. God the Father then tells Holy Spirit, "I love my people so completely that I not only sent my Son to die so they never have to, but now I will send you to direct them in everything, and to comfort them and bring them peace. This will make it possible for them to live the abundant life. I not only want them to have life, but have it to the full." (John 10:10).

Jesus made it possible for us to have the gift of eternal life, and Holy Spirit is hope alive in every work of our life. He was sent to teach us and remind us of Jesus, and all He did and said as He worked out the Father's plan. This is how we know we will be able to accomplish all that God has set out for us to do, because the Holy Spirit reminds us of the witness of Jesus. Jesus tells the disciples in John 24:29 that they will be "clothed with power from on high." 1 Corinthians 2 tells us God has prepared wonderful things for us and the Holy Spirit reveals them to us because He searches all things—the deep things of God. (See 1 Corinthians 2: 6-16). This is why we need to invite the Holy Spirit as our Ultimate Life-Consultant. He really does have all the answers.

*Dear God you have given us a divine handbook for life. We don't always interpret it or apply it to the fullest, this is why you sent the Holy Spirit as our Counselor. He provides deeper insight into the life and mission of Jesus. We have to fully understand His work, to fully understand our own. We are grateful that you have something unique for all of us to complete while we are on earth. We want to complete it with the Spirit's guiding and insight so that it is fully pleasing to you. We give you our minds, our hearts and our hands as we wait for your directives.*

*In Jesus' name we pray. Amen.*

## PRAYING PROPHETICALLY TO WORK THE PLAN

Amos 3:7 (NIV) Surely, the Sovereign Lord does nothing without revealing His plan to His servants the prophets.

What is your personal prophecy? Everyone is a prophet in his own right, in his own life. We speak what we will be: "I am blessed" or "I am stressed." We either pronounce "I don't know what God's will is," or, "I will pray, search and seek and wait upon the Lord to show me the way because He said He would never leave me or forsake me."

As we serve the Lord we must listen for His voice. As we pray and read the Word to prepare ourselves and anticipate the day's events, the day's gifts, the day's responsibilities, and the day's signs, we must heed His voice. Every day there is a plan and purpose. As we run our daily race, how do we know the course? We pray and listen so we can find God's cadence. We take notice of what He is telling us to walk out and to speak. What is your daily testimony? Your personal life's prophecy?

God spoke to me as I was praying with Him and writing this and He said: "You have to talk the talk, to walk the walk," meaning we have to declare divine truths over our life to come to know the abundant life and live it well.

Are your words and actions bringing you closer or farther away from your destiny; from God's plan?

2 Peter (NIV) For prophecy never had its origin in the human will, but prophets, though human, spoke from God as they were carried along by the Holy Spirit.

God has set something in motion in your inner man, which is being awakened and drawn up and out of you. Your words can help produce the fruit of the plan and purpose, or they can squelch it.

God has been forming you physically and spiritually since before you were a thought on anyone's mind, known only to Him. He has been with you since your beginning. This is why you can trust Him with what He has whispered to you. He has revealed

His plan about you and to you.

Let's pray prophetically together:

*Dear wonderful Father, we come today to say that we believe what you have spoken to us through your Son, your Word, and through others about who we are and the plan you have for us. We declare that we will cooperate with you and move only where the Spirit tells us to go. We thank you for the divine promises sent to each of us. We believe that what you have spoken to us, for you are not a man that you should lie. We agree with these promises and that you will supply all we need as we work with you to bring about our whole selves—who you intended us to be—as we give you glory. May our prayers be ones filled with words of prophecy that carry us along by the Holy Spirit.*

*In Jesus' name we pray. Amen.*

# REWARD

## I'M CALLING YOU

Philippians 3:13-14 (NIV): Brothers and sisters, I do not consider myself yet to have taken hold of it. But one thing I do: Forgetting what is behind and straining toward what is ahead, I press on toward the goal to win the prize for which God has *called* me heavenward in Christ Jesus."
(Italics mine.)

When God calls, if we have the right spirit within us, it's always good news. Why would we ever want to miss a call from God? Unfortunately, we do, often. I know I do. But, we can begin to be more available and invested in our life-line to God, which is our prayer time. What we say to God and what we hear Him saying is the basis of our relationship with Him. Isn't communication key to every relationship?

Receiving the upward call happens when we say "yes" to Jesus, and it continues as we set out to live a life worthy of the call that is talked about in Ephesians 4:1.

How do we know if we are living a life worthy of the upward call? We pray and read the Word. As we pray, God can share the specifics about our call. I think most of us get the "big picture" of the worthy life. You know, love God and others; but how to do this is found out as we meditate in the Word and continue to develop our prayer life. I believe the specifics about your own unique, worthy calling is often laid out to you in your prayer closet and then confirmed in the Word. Again, we have a relational God, and He is calling you into deeper communion with Him.

Do you cry out to Him for revelation of His plan and purpose? Are you answering any calls? Is He getting your "voicemail" much of the time? If so, you aren't making Him first and He is not the master of your time. If you knew that God was going to call you today at five o'clock, would you make sure to be available? I am certain we would all answer "yes!" to that question. But many times He has called us and had to leave a message. The messages may sound like this:

"While you were out, I tried to help you solve that problem at work."

"While you were out I came by to tell you a wonderful secret and give you a gift that I have hidden in my heart for you until the right time, but you missed it because you weren't home."

He is our home and someday we will live in eternity with Him and share in all the wonders He has for us, but we can experience that now a little bit each time we answer the call. When we go to Him in prayer; this is where we will find our reward.

*Dear Lord, we love you. We thank you. We praise you. How wonderful that you want to talk to us as the church, as your bride, to help us fulfill our calling—the upward call. How marvelous that you want to talk to us about our personal gifts and calling. It's amazing to us that you are only a whisper away: every day, every hour, every minute. At a moment's notice we can call out and you will draw near to us. You are continuously calling out to us, and to all creation. As we go through this time in prayer with you, may we have a deeper revelation as the church, as your bride, and individually. Lord, you are our reward. Let us pray Matthew 6:6 together:*

"But you, when you pray, go into your room and when you have shut your door, pray to your Father who is in the secret place, and your Father who sees in secret will reward you openly."

(The following section was written during Pastor Appreciation Month.)

### PRAYERS OF BLESSING ARE A REWARD

Have you ever been blessed by someone and you knew they really meant it? It's a reward like no other. Or, have you ever blessed someone with such intentionality that you knew it would happen? You knew there was "weight" in what you said because it came straight from the Father, through you, to accomplish His good work in that blessing. I believe one of the best representations of Jesus' love is to bless someone.

Last week, a well-known visiting minister spoke at New Hope about positioning yourself for a miracle. There are things you have to do to be in position. When we talk about reward as mentioned in Philippians 3:13-14, it brings a "God-thought" to mind: when you press on, you are positioning yourself for the reward. New Hope is a church that is in position for reward, for miracles, because our pastor and those who serve alongside him have positioned themselves to receive these things.

It is a blessing and reward to belong to a place of worship that has authentic, righteous leadership. It's a blessing that deserves reciprocation.

Pray for your pastor. Pray prayers of blessings upon your leadership. Sharing Jesus' love with your pastor is just as important as sharing it with people outside the church walls. Take the opportunity to bless them with all sincerity of heart. Do this so your leaders can get into a position to receive this blessing of goodness. Pastors need to be filled up because they have to continually pour out.

Pastor's Blessing:

*We bless you with a Hebrews 13:17 joy: that you would have joy and not grief as you continue to watch and care for other's souls.*

*We bless you with a 1 Thessalonians 5:12-13 blessing. We bless you and hold you in high esteem in love for your work's sake. We bless you with a flock that is at peace with one another.*

*We bless you with a life and ministry that lives out the Gospel. (1 Corinthians 9:14)*

*We bless you with a Romans 15:13 blessing: That you would be filled with all joy and peace in believing and that you may abound in hope by the power of the Holy Spirit.*

*We bless your time.*

*We bless you with excellent health.*

*We bless your marriage and relationships—that they may flourish.*

*We bless your work, whether it be accomplished through your mind or hands.*

*We bless your coming and your going.*

*We bless your present and your future.*

*We bless your life and the prophecies yet to come to pass. We call them forth with a blessing attached.*

*We bless you with all the tools and strategies you need in this time.*

*We bless you with holiness, righteousness, wisdom, and power in Christ Jesus to accomplish the works prepared in advance for you to do.*

*We bless your secret heart's desires that are known by you and your heavenly Father. May you be blessed in your innermost being.*

*We bless you with strength and grace.*

*We bless you and your position as pastor.*

*You are a great gift and we thank God for you. In Jesus' name. Amen.*

## PRAYERS THAT PRODUCE A REWARD

Your prayers have the potential to turn your greatest need into your greatest reward.

Imagine that the difficulty you are going through right now could be turned upside down and pour a blessing and reward upon you.

This is possible with prayers: prayers that bring recognition to the Father, prayers that recognize the absolute power in Jesus, and prayers that realize Holy Spirit is a constant guide and source of wisdom. These are the prayers that need to be prayed concerning that specific thing that is your greatest need, or that place within you (or someone else) that needs filling or refreshing. Your prayers and your words have great *potential*. They are the *inertia* that moves your Father's heart and hand. Isaiah 58:9a (NKJV):

> Then you shall call and the Lord will answer; you shall cry and He will say, "Here I am."

There are many rewards that can come from a trial or walking in adversity, but let's briefly examine two.

One of these rewards is a deeper friendship with God. Abraham was a friend of God. He must have gone through a great testing when God was about to destroy Sodom and Gomorrah, because he asked God to spare a sinful city. God answered each prayer and petition that Abraham prayed. Imagine if Abraham would have prayed one more time, with fewer righteous ones in his request to spare Sodom and Gomorrah? This account would lead us to believe that Abraham knew God answered prayer, especially those of His friends.

Another reward found within our troubles is our testimony. This is our overcoming of the enemy. We overcome by the blood of the Lamb and the word of our testimony. Our lives consist of a series of testimonies, don't they? And Jesus tells us in Revelation 22:12,

> "Behold I am coming quickly, and my reward is with

me, to render to every man according to what he has done." Jesus is returning to reward us according to our testimonies.

Let's pray.

*Lord, we recognize you are sovereign over our lives. Our very act of praying indicates your sovereignty. May we invite you into our circumstances so that in your infinite goodness and authority you can work on our behalf. Jesus, your sacrifice holds all the power we need; even over death. Holy Spirit, you are the wise voice that tells us how to graciously live and move and have our being in God. We believe our prayers reach you and you respond. Show us how to pray. We specifically invite you into our current difficulties that we may proclaim your truth and promises, which will turn the tide of adversity into swells of triumph. We believe that out of these hardships will be a greater friendship as we abide in you, and a testimony that declares us victorious. We purpose ourselves this day to pray prayers with great potential. To pray in a way that produces a reward, and we will do all of this in Jesus' powerful name. Amen!*

# ENDNOTES

1       https://www.nbcnews.com/news/us-news/kentucky-gives-blessing-bible-classes-public-school-n777721
2       https://www.christian-headlines.com/blog/please-pray-for-us-asks-politician-as-congress-addresses-sexual-harassment.html
3       https://www1.cbn.com/cbnnews/cwn/2017/november/european-christians-march-against-lsquo-christianophobia-rsquo-after-court-rules-to-remove-cross-from-statue
4       https://www.christianitytoday.com/news/2017/october/pence-us-persecuted-christians-usaid-un.html
5       https://www.whitehouse.gov/briefings-statements/statement-president-trump-jerusalem/
6       https://www1.cbn.com/cbnnews/entertainment/2017/november/mariah-carey-featured-in-new-christian-christmas-film-the-star
7       https://www.google.com/search?q=reflect+definition&rlz=1C1CHBF_enUS866US866&oq=reflect+definition&aqs=chrome..69i57j0l7.4113j1j8&sourceid=chrome&ie=UTF-8

# 3

# Prayers of *Life*

# WRECKED

## PRAYERS OF INTERSECTION

Lately, I have been pondering the concept of an intersection where two roads—two thoughts or revelations—meet.

Are you praying prayers of intersection? Jesus Himself is an intersection: He is the son of man and the Son of God. Jesus the son of man was and is sinless; while on earth He never said a bad word about anyone, never lied, never gave up on the mission, never disobeyed His parents. He never did anything the Father didn't tell Him to do.

> John 5:19 (NIV) "Very truly I tell you, the son can do nothing by himself; he can only do what He sees the father doing, because whatever the father does the son does also."

It is powerful to realize this truth about Jesus—He was not just clothed in full humanity, but He was fully human. He was like us, yet sinless. This truth does make Him the perfect example; the perfect atoning sacrifice. He is the perfect way out of our own humanity; we are made new and not bound by our sin nature. Here is some good news that we find in 1 Corinthians 10:13 (GNT):

> Every test that you have experienced is the kind that normally comes to people. But, God keeps His promise, and He will not allow you to be tested beyond your power to remain firm. At the time you were tested, He will give you strength to endure it and provide you a way out.

The way out is Jesus.

Becoming the son of man wasn't just a "time out" from being the Son of God for thirty-three years. It was our living, saving grace; our living hope; our living holiness. This is what makes Jesus a bonified Savior. He lived as a man, which means we are able to trust that He not only saved us, but understands us. He alone is purity, perfection, and love. Jesus' holiness is something to be an awe of every day.

Isaiah tells of his own experience when he encountered God's holiness in Isaiah chapter 6. He speaks about the glory of God filling the earth and how this revelation of God made him feel unworthy or undone. Some, in present day, might use the term "wrecked."

Jesus as the Son of God is the second part of the intersection. Jesus was with God from the beginning. He was always the Son of God. When Jesus walked the earth, the glory that Isaiah was speaking of was manifested in Jesus—the son of man.

What if someone said to you, "I know a man. He comes from the wealthiest family in the Kingdom. He never did anything wrong. He is the kindest person you will ever meet. He is powerful. He can save you from anything; even death. He is handsome with kind eyes, creative and insightful. He truly understands you in every way. He speaks of love; yet He is love. Oh, and by the way, He wants to meet you." Wouldn't you be awestruck and amazed? Maybe wrecked? And this would all be before you came to know that He is also part of the Triune God! Imagine how it would be when you had the encounter of the wholeness of who this man was; when you came to the intersection of Jesus as the Son of God and Jesus as the Son of Man. Let us stay at this intersection for a while because it will surely bring about a greater place of wonder and awe about our complete and perfect Savior.

Let's pray a prayer of intersection.

*Jesus, we thank you for your amazing sacrifice. We are in awe that we have a perfect and complete Savior in you. You are the only way out, our rescue from what tempts us. But, what peace we have, knowing we can trust you entirely because you understand us in our humanity fully, and you also understand the Father completely. You are the intersection in which we should stand, the place where earthly and heavenly meet.*

*Oh, Jesus, the Son of Man and the Son of God—the perfect man and the perfect God that we love. We stand amazed and in a place of admiration of you are and what you have accomplished for us.*

*We want to see you fully. Help us. In Jesus' name. Amen*

## ARE YOU PRAYING AT THE WHEEL?

Ezekiel chapters 1 and 10 speak of a wheel and paints a picture of the heavenly encounter Ezekiel had with the glory of God. The four wheels that were beside and working with each of the four angels, which were under the glory of God or the Throne of Grace, had eyes all over them. These wheels were surveying the Earth. This encounter had to change Ezekiel forever! It was here that Ezekiel ate the word of God, which at that time were words of woe for the Israelites. However, the Spirit of God came upon Ezekiel and brought him to his feet. The Spirit of God allowed Ezekiel to eat God's bitter message. It was a message of destruction, yet Ezekiel said it tasted of honey.

If we allow the Spirit of God to visit us; He will raise us up and even carry us to where we need to go and do what God is calling us to do. (Ezekiel says the Spirit carried him to the Kebar River, where he sat overwhelmed for seven days.)

After the seven days, God returned to Ezekiel and gave him words to prophesy to Israel. God was going to make Himself known to Israel. He was prepared to do what he had to do bring about the change and repentance of His people. God was about to wreck Israel's current way of rebellious life. One definition of "wreck" is "completely spoil."

God will completely spoil our idea of life and how we think it should look. We could also say He will destroy our selfishness and sin within us to be sure He can dwell in and among us. God goes to the extreme to do this; just read Ezekiel and you will see this is true. God wrecked Israel to bring her back to Him, and He wrecked Ezekiel so he was sold out to Him. .

Ezekiel had an encounter that he couldn't ignore or shake. This prayer line between God and Ezekiel, concerning Israel, went on for twenty-two years. Ezekiel prayed at the wheel for twenty-two years because he could not forget the glory of God. You might feel like you have been praying for change within yourself or someone else, maybe in your family, or within our nation for many years and it's becoming hard to hold onto the wheel of prayer. But, remember, that at the end of Ezekiel the temple was rebuilt, and

the city's name was forever to be, "The Lord is there."
Let us pray at the wheel together.

*Lord, we are in awe of you. You are all-knowing and all-seeing. Your eyes are searching for those who want to follow you. Thank you that you are an all-consuming God and you are jealous for us to the point of destruction; the destruction that brings about full repentance and creates a place that you can live and dwell among us. Help us to remember when we are at the wheel of prayer that you see it all and are working on our behalf. Let your glory fall on our lives because we are in a place of surrender. Help those of us amid trials to remember that if we believe, in faith, you will turn the situation around because you are at the wheel with us. In Jesus' name. Amen*

## ONE TO MANY...

Isaiah 51: 2 (NLT) "Yes, think about Abraham, your ancestor, and Sarah, who gave birth to your nation. Abraham was only one man when I called him. But when I blessed him, he became a great nation."

Have you prayed for one thing? Let's say a child, or a home, or a healing, or even a miracle. And it turned into many?

For example, when you pray for a child you are thinking about that one blessing of the baby (Psalm 127:3) but then we see there are many blessings deposited within that person's life; perhaps even thousands.

Think of a time you were healed or had a miracle. You were thinking about how wonderful it would be to be without that pain or limitation in your body or mind, which was one blessing; but now when you think of that answered prayer and how much goodness came from it, you see many blessings. Perhaps others were touched by your experience and they had the faith to receive for themselves. Possibly those you met along the way, as you were seeking your healing, were touched and changed by your witness. I believe that at first Abraham and Sarah were focused on the blessing of their promised child. It was, most likely, difficult for them to think of the millions of blessings that would come from the one blessing of Isaac.

As I was writing this, the phrase "one to many" kept coming to my mind. Don't confuse this with the saying, "one too many." I came across a definition on Techopedia's website that explains this phrase, which I didn't know existed. It has to do with databases. "One to many" is a relationship that can be found within a relational database. "A relational database is a type of database that stores and provides access to data points that are related to one another. Relational databases are based on the relational model, an intuitive, straightforward way of representing data in tables. In a relational database, each row in the table is a record with a unique ID called the key. The columns of the table hold attributes of the data, and each record usually has a value for each attribute, making it easy to establish the relationships among data points." The term "one to many" refers to the fact that a parent record on one table can reference several child records on another table. Techopedia went on to explain it like this: "The one-to-many relationship is only a principle of database design, which cannot be explicitly defined in the database structure. Instead, it is implicitly created and enforced by the use of relationships between tables, especially the relationship between a primary key and a foreign key." [1]

The technical definition of "one to many" sounds very much like a term, or phrase, we might hear as we are reading the Bible. Words like, "parent," "child," "relationship," and "table" remind us of the family of God. So, let's think this way: One blessing—or record, if we are speaking technically—can affect many other records; even change a table. We can think of a database table, or a literal table within a home. Think of how the parent/child interaction at one dinner table influences the next generation's table. Imagine how Abraham and Sarah's table changed countless tables throughout history. So, one person, one blessing, one answered prayer, or one miracle can turn into many by the hand of God. May we not miss the many for the one.

Shall we pray?

*Lord, you are infinite. You have more than we could ever imagine. We are realizing that when you do something it is more complete, meaningful, lasting, and influential than we even know. You are always showing us that you take our prayers from good to great; our lives from good to great; our blessings from one to many. It's like you are wrecking us at every turn. Lord, today we thank you for one answered prayer that turned into many. We are grateful to you that you always give above what we ask; even above what we need.*

*In Jesus' name we pray. Amen*

## MAKE WAY FOR THE GLORY SEASON

Aren't we all heading to a new place? If we believe this, we should ask ourselves: Are our prayers helping carry us there or are they hindering our arrival at our divine destination? Are you speaking the word of truth—the God-breathed Scriptures over your path? Are you listening for God's heart speaking to you while you pray? Maybe He has spoken a rhema word to you—a personal word just to you, for you and about you. If we have heard this word, or we hope for one, we should awaken to the signs along the prayer path. God gave New Hope Church, and each one of us, indivicually, a rhema word.

> Zechariah 2:5 (NKJV): "For I," says the Lord, "will be a wall of fire all around her, and I will be the glory in her midst."

We can usher in the glory of the Lord or we can subdue it with absent-minded and half-hearted prayers; prayers that lack faith and life. But God is telling us this *rhema* word in this hour to usher in the next wave of His presence so he can take us where we all know we want to be: in the glory season.

> Isaiah 40:1-5 (NKJV): "Comfort, yes, comfort My people!" says your God. Speak comfort to Jerusalem, and cry out to her, that her warfare is ended, that her iniquity is pardoned; for she has received from the Lord's hand double for all her sins. The voice of one crying in the wilderness: Prepare the way of the Lord; make straight in the desert a highway for our God. Every valley shall be exalted and every mountain and hill brought low; the crooked places shall be made straight and the rough places smooth; the glory of the Lord shall be revealed, and all flesh shall see it together; for the mouth of the Lord has spoken."

These words tell us that we cannot stay where we are. We must take hold of the truths of our victory over sin and death.

# Prayers of Life

The price has been paid for us to live the victorious life and pray victorious prayers. Those of us who are struggling with sin need to be reminded to pray and ask when we should turn to the left or to the right, so that we may avoid wrecking into it. We need to ask how to fully rely on God for the next directive, or how to navigate "the bends" in the road. We don't have to know the entire route right now; we just need to stay on the course. Isaiah 40: 1-5 tells us to prepare the highway for Him, so that He can reach us and become the glory in our midst, because we have prepared the way for Him.

Let's pray a prayer together that beckons to our God and His glory. Let us lift our voices and say,

*"Come Lord, and show us how to prepare ourselves and our churches, so that you can come and be a wall of fire around us and be the glory within. Thank you for the comfort we have in knowing that you have given us a way out of our sin, and through our repentance we can begin to see that our prayers of victory will make a way for you.*

*Let our words and the meditations of our hearts urge you closer so that every valley shall be raised up and every mountain and hill made low, the rough ground level, and the rugged places a plain. And then your glory will be revealed, and all of us together will see it. For your mouth, oh Lord, has spoken. We believe in Jesus' name. Amen.*

## NO GRAVES

### MIRACLES IN THE DARK.

God can resurrect the dead places in the dark; and He does. Are you praying in the dark?

Our God is a god of resurrection. He is not only a God of revival and revitalization; He is a God of resurrection in the dark!

John 20:1 tells us that Mary Magdalene went to the tomb while it was still dark to find that the tomb had been rolled away. This means the greatest miracle of all time occurred in the dark right before dawn!

The darkness can mean different things to each of us. Maybe to one person it's the unknown, or to another questions of the heart. It could be the shame of secret sin, or misery from sickness; the despair of lost joy, or anguish in a difficult relationship.

Darkness represents an arduous situation—a time of waiting for light, waiting for resurrection. Your darkness has you sitting in a grave. But, God is the ultimate grave robber! Aren't you grateful that He robbed you from the grave of sin and death? This isn't our only resurrection, however; and it is our prayers that invite God to act on our behalf for victories and deliverances along the way. God has decreed that you are dead to the old self, to lusts, envy, fear, sickness, etc., and alive to who you are in CHRIST. You are a new creation, a new person with self-control, joy, compassion and an indwelling of the Holy Spirit.

God will rob you from every grave, and from the grip of the enemy, if you let Him. Start looking for your resurrections. God wants to remove the darkness from every area of our lives. Therefore, we must pray prayers of resurrection, especially when we find ourselves in the tomb. Just imagine Jesus in the dark tomb and suddenly, just before dawn, the greatest light of all time shone for the world and for eternity to see.

For the first time, I see 1 Corinthians 4:5 (NIV) differently:

Therefore, judge nothing before the appointed time; wait until the Lord comes. He will bring to light what is hidden in the darkness and will expose the motives of the heart. At that time each will receive their praise from God.

If you consider this verse in light of the resurrection of Jesus happening in the dark, it takes on a different meaning. Sometimes we miss the miracle or the resurrection of something and so, we miss the Father's heart. His heart is always fixed on life. Let's begin asking in prayer for God to show us the miracles that are taking place in the darkness.

*Father, we give our dark places to you—our sins, our unbelief, our pride—our tombs. We see the enemy's undoing as we give ourselves to you. Cause us to see what is taking place in the dark, so truth will be illuminated and set us free in these areas. May not one grave remain. Forgive us, Lord, for thinking these resurrections are less important than the Resurrection, because that was your purpose in bringing Jesus from death to life—so that we may live the resurrection life. Let our prayers be declarations of light and life, full of faith, so that even when it is dark and we are in the graveyard, we contend in the dark and look for the light, which is the work that you are doing. That is when the dawn will come.*

*Thank you for the abundant life. We cannot remain dead. We must rise to the occasion, so we can be set free in all areas of our lives. We may be walking step-by-step in the dark, but we know if we trust you, we will be lifted high above the grave and darkness until full resurrection comes! Thank you that you are mighty to save. Praise you for the greatest miracle that happened in the dark—the big one, that brought about the Light and Hope of all the world: Jesus. Amen.*

## THOUGHTS AND PRAYERS FOR THE ABUNDANT LIFE

Our quality of life depends on our thoughts. Proverbs 3:7 tells us "As a man thinketh, so is he."

Our thoughts develop our attitudes, our attitudes develop our words, and our words develop our lives.

We really should consider everything we say a prayer, especially if we have asked Jesus to be our Lord and Savior; if we acknowledge God, we must acknowledge that He dwells within us.

2 Corinthians 6:16 (NIV) tells us:

"I will live in them and walk among them. I will be their God and they will be my people."

When we speak, our words may not be intentional prayer; but all that we do, we do unto the Lord.

Isaiah 66:1 (NAS 77): Thus saith the Lord, "Heaven is my throne, and earth is my footstool. Where then is a house you could build me? And where is a place I may rest?"

God is everywhere: omnipresent. We know that He lives in us. This must mean He is a part of every conversation. Don't make God live among poor thoughts, attitudes, and words. Make His house (the temple of the Holy Spirit that is you), come alive with thoughts and words that cultivate goodness. Let all your thoughts be seeds of righteousness, and let your attitudes and your words water those seeds, producing a rich and abundant harvest—the good life that God intended for you.

1 Corinthians 2:9-12 (NKJV): But as it is written: "Eye has not seen, nor ear heard, nor have entered into the heart of man the things which God has prepared for those who love Him. But God has revealed them to us through His Spirit. For the Spirit searches all things, yes, the deep things of God. For what man knows the things of a man except the spirit of the man which is in him? Even so no one knows the things of God except the Spirit of God. Now we have

received, not the spirit of the world, but the Spirit who is from God, that we might know the things that have been freely given to us by God."

When we speak the truth, we are exercising our faith.

*Lord, there are unimaginable riches waiting for us. Riches so wonderful that only the Spirit knows them. Your Word tells us we have received your Spirit, and the Spirit of God knows the thoughts of God. This is a wonderful mystery to us. It means that we have access to the thoughts of God! We are able to have "God thoughts" in every situation.*

*Lord, as we do this more and more and realize you have a good, even miraculous, outcome for every situation, we will truly be living the abundant life. May the Spirit of God, whom we have received, begin to reveal the mind of God, the thoughts of the Father to us. Lord, we thank you for your wondrous gift of your Spirit. In Jesus' name we pray. Amen.*

## ARISE AND SHINE-PRAYERS THAT LIFT

If we are lifted up, we are most definitely above the grave. Prayers are meant to lift us. This happens as we raise up our God, as we exalt Him, and then we are lifted as well because we are in Him. If we acknowledge that we are in Him, then as we lift His name in prayer and praise, exalting Him above our lives and circumstances, we will be lifted to a higher place.

> Colossians 1:27-28 (NIV): To them God has chosen to make known among the Gentiles the glorious riches of this mystery, which is in Christ in you the hope of glory. We proclaim Him admonishing and teaching everyone with all wisdom so that we may present everyone perfect in Christ. To this end I labor, struggling with all His energy which so powerfully works in me."

It is God's power that raises us above the grave. These are lifting prayers. Lift is a verb meaning "raise to a higher position or level."

> 1 Corinthians (NLT): "And God will raise us from the dead by His power, just as He raised our Lord from the dead."

A second definition of lift is "to pick up and move to another position."

> Ephesians 2:6 (NLT): For He raised us up from the dead along with Christ and seated us with Him in the heavenly realm because we are united with Christ Jesus.

A third definition of lift is "raise, encourage or cheer."

> Isaiah 60:1: Arise and shine for your light has come and the glory of the Lord rises upon you.

A fourth definition is to "formally remove or end a legal restriction."

> Romans 6:14 (NLT): Sin is no longer your master, for you no longer live under the requirements of the law instead you live under the freedom of God's grace.

Now let's look at lift as a noun. One definition is a "free ride in someone else's vehicle." We took a free ride on Jesus's atoning sacrifice for our sins. And another definition is the "force that directly opposes the weight of an airplane and holds the airplane in the air." God's love is the force that opposes the weight of this life and keeps us above our circumstances. His wings protect us and if we rest there, they will lift us.

> Deuteronomy 32:11 (NASB): Like an eagle that stirs up its nest, That hovers over its young, He spread His wings and caught them, He carried them on His pinions.

*Lord, we acknowledge you are the lifter of our souls. We set you high above everything. May there be nothing in our lives or within us that competes with you and your rightful place. We exalt your name—Yahweh, I Am that I Am, the Alpha and the Omega, the Creator, the King of kings and the Lord of lords. You are the force that raises us from every grave in our lives. As you lift us we find shelter under your wings. We acknowledge that your power is what heals us, strengthens us, and guides us. Lift our infirmities as we praise you and lift you high. May our faith be lifted, and cause us to arise so that we may receive you fully. In Jesus' name. Amen.*

# I AM WHO GOD SAYS I AM

## GET BUSY BEING YOU

In Matthew 16: 13-19 Jesus is asking the disciples to state who He is.

> When Jesus came to the region of Caesarea Philippi, He asked His disciples, "Who do people say the Son of Man is? They replied, "Some say John the Baptist; others say Elijah; and still others, Jeremiah or one of the prophets.""But what about you?" He asked. "Who do you say I am?" Simon Peter answered, "You are the Messiah, the Son of the living God."

> Jesus replied, "Blessed are you, Simon son of Jonah, for this was not revealed to you by flesh and blood, but by my Father in heaven. And I tell you that you are Peter, and on this rock I will build my church, and the gates of Hades will not overcome it. I will give you the keys of the kingdom of heaven; whatever you bind on earth will be bound in heaven, and whatever you loose on earth will be loosed in heaven."

So, this is where Simon becomes Peter. He became his true self once he openly confessed who the Son of Man was. Jesus told him that this understanding was not revealed to him by man, but by the Father.

This speaks to us and our identity. No man or woman can tell us who we are, nor should we let any worldly ideologies or philosophies define us. Once Simon spoke the truth about who Jesus was, he was immediately given a new name, and Jesus proclaimed He would build the Church upon the Rock of Peter's faith and profession. And, Peter and the Church would be given the keys to the Kingdom. Jesus also spoke about the power and

# Prayers of Life

authority we possess in Christ. This isn't just true for Simon Peter, but it is for all of us. The more we realize who Jesus is, the bigger revelation we have of who we are. If you feel you have no identity, or don't know your purpose, start praying for a deeper revelation of Jesus. That is where you will find Him and yourself. Prayer and the Word are the vehicles we use to search out how we are to be known—to discover our heavenly identity.

Peter was a disciple and he spent all his time in the presence of the Word incarnate (Jesus). We could say Peter's daily life consisted of prayer and the Word. Our lives may not look exactly like Peter's, but we do have the opportunity to pray every day.

God wants us to know who we are. One day, about fifteen years ago, as I was praying the Holy Spirit spoke to me and said, "Get busy being you." This was His answer to a prayer. (I had been praying about some difficult relationships in my life. What God was saying was I just needed to be open and honest with myself and with others.) So, I had to let God guide me in becoming a more authentic *me*. When you allow God to be your leader you will become your true self. When God is your leader, He takes you somewhere; becoming your truest self is a journey. It would be wonderful if it happened instantly at salvation, but it doesn't. As we seek out the identity of Jesus and follow Him, we begin to see who He is and who we are in Him.

So, my response to God when He spoke to my heart was: "Lord, show me the truth about myself and who I am in this situation." This is an effective prayer to pray in all circumstances . It is a "firewall" against the enemy, declaring that I won't forget who I am in any situation. Praying for this truth is powerful, because it always points to our wholeness, to us become our complete selves. And, we must also remember to consider who Jesus is for us at all times, and then specifically for what we are currently facing. We know that Jesus is all things powerful and righteous, but He may be the grace we need to be gracious in a difficult season. Can you remember a time when Jesus was your ___(fill in the blank)_____, during a trial or hardship? That was your truth for that situation and as you let the Holy Spirit guide you, you become more __(fill in the blank)_____.

Let's pray for your current season and situation. How does it look to be fully you? Let's get busy being our true selves.

*Lord, show us the truth about who you are as you continue to lead us from where we are, right now. And, we know as you do, we will begin to see your truth shine forth upon us, illuminating who we are. Just like Simon, we declare that you are the Christ, the Son of the living God. As we declare this truth over our lives and our situations, we will begin to see you and who we are in you.*

*John 8:36 says, "If the Son sets you free, you will be free indeed." We declare this over our lives as we become free to be who you created us to be. You may not give us a new name (in this life, anyway), but you will build something upon us and our lives. You will give us keys and authority in you. Lord, you told Peter you would use him, but the conversation didn't stop there; we have to believe that you continued to speak to Peter as he grew in ministry and as he faced trials and triumphs of all kinds. So, in this truth, we recognize that you have told us many things, and you will bring your purposes to their completion as we profess the truth of who are and what you reveal to us about ourselves.*

*Thank you for setting us free and giving us keys to open doors: doors to health, provision, righteousness, victorious living, peace, contentment, joy, miracles, signs and wonders. Lord, you are all these blessings, and so much more. We know that if we choose to live in you, we are these attributes as well. We believe in the Truth that sets us free. We pray this in the name of Truth: in the name of Jesus. Amen.*

## WHO AM I?

When we begin to get interested in what God wants us to do, we become busy with the Kingdom. This isn't the same as worldly busyness, but is a joyful enterprise utilizing the gifts God has given us, producing fruit. God gives gifts, and as we use them to glorify Him, we grow the fruit within our lives. So, don't be deceived that Kingdom work is overwhelming or something to add to the "to-do" list. Once you have the truth residing in you about your call, it actually feeds your soul, unlike frantic worldly activity that can overwhelm and crowd out our true self. This is true because when we respond to God, we are practicing obedience. Our obedience answers the call of God, but it also answers the question, "Who am I?"

God asks us to heed His voice and when we do, in His completeness as the Author and Perfecter of our lives, He gives greater clarity to us about our gifts, talents, and dreams, because they are all tied to what He is calling us to. When we obey God, we become our truest selves.

When we pray we should remember how intimately God knows us. He doesn't separate who we are from our call, which is where He is leading us. When God is your leader, He takes you somewhere. As we answer the Kingdom call, given to us through the Word and the Holy Spirit, we begin to understand our God, our Savior, and the person of the Holy Spirit in a tangible way. This is how we see and know ourselves truly. We are created in God's likeness. As we become more like our leader, we become more like ourselves.

*Lord, thank you that we are called by you. Romans 8:30 tells us that you predestined us, called us, justified us, and glorified us. Help us to walk in a manner worthy of the calling. We thank you that you go before us, leading us on paths of righteousness for your name's sake. Thank you, Lord, that you are the most worthy leader. This is how we are assured in our journey, and can press on toward the goal for the prize of the upward call of God in Christ Jesus. (Philippians 3:14).*

Lord, we come to know and answer the question; "Who am I?" as we answer the call, because we are in you. John 10:3 tells us the doorkeeper opens the door of the sheep pen, and the sheep hear His voice, and He calls his own sheep by name and leads them out. Thank you, Lord, for all that you do. We are your sheep and we do hear your voice. In Jesus' name we pray. Amen.

# ENDNOTES

1   https://www.techopedia.com/definition/25122/one-to-many-relationship

# 4

# Prayers of Triumph

# HEAVEN STEPS

### WORDS THAT MOVE

The words we speak can bring us a lot closer to heaven…or not.

What's in your mouth? Have you ever asked a toddler this question? I believe God says this to us regarding our prayer lives. So, what is in your mouth? Is it words and sounds from heaven? It should be.

We usually pray to God because we need to be saved from something. Think of a simple prayer before we start our day. It may sound a little like this, "Lord, I want to put you first today. Help me to show others more of you and not me. Save others and myself from me!"

So we might pray about being saved from a bad day, or being saved from insanity in a crazy world, or saved from calamity, or saved from a parking ticket during a one-and-a-half hour lunch break; whatever it may be, our words have power. Our prayers mean something.

Do you believe your words have power to help or hurt, to raise or lower your effectiveness in your situation? If you declare with your mouth Jesus is Lord and believe in your heart that God raised him from the dead, you will be saved (Romans 10:9). This passage speaks about our salvation from eternal damnation and separation from God, but this is also a promise that holds true in every situation that speaks to our needing salvation.

So—consider something you need to be saved from. Begin to profess that Jesus is Lord over that situation and the same power that God used to raise our Savior, His Son, from the dead is available to us. It is at work on our behalf, if we speak it out—if heaven is in our mouths! If we begin to do this, then our hearts will hear our mouths profess Jesus' lordship over our lives, and it will begin to believe in this resurrection power. We will begin to believe in our hearts that anything is possible. It is true that we usually speak from the overflow of our hearts, but I believe that often we must speak truth to our hearts so that more truth will come forth. But remember that our hearts can deceive us, so get ahead of your heart and speak out heavenly words, so that your heart will hear them and begin to fuel more Kingdom talk.

Let's speak the words of heaven together. Shall we pray?

*Lord, we acknowledge Jesus as Lord and Savior over us and over our lives. We bring this situation that needs saving to you, and we speak to it, declaring "Jesus is Lord" over it. God, you are working on our behalf with the greatest power—the power of resurrection. We profess that no power under heaven has influence over us or this situation. We declare John 16:33, that in this world we will have trouble, but we can take heart because you have overcome the world. This tells us that if we speak heaven from our lips, each word will be words of triumph with the promise to overcome. We declare 1 John 5: 4-5: that those who overcome the world are those that believe that Jesus is the Son of God. For whatever is born of God overcomes the world, and this is the victory that has overcome the world, our faith.*

*Lord, may we be faithful in speaking truth, and having heaven on our hearts and minds and lips. May we praise you forevermore. Amen.*

## WALK ON THROUGH.

Are you like Paul, waiting for God to physically release you from a prison of some sort? Acts 5:19 tells us during the night an Angel of the Lord opened the doors of the jail and brought them out.

When God opens a door we should step through it. When we do, it releases us into a new place—maybe a new anointing, a new calling, a new job, a new opportunity, a new ministry; or maybe to a place of peace or healing.

Sometimes we are holding onto things that are keeping us from an open door. Have you ever known that God was taking you somewhere? You could see the path, and knew the door was ahead; but you didn't continue on the ancient path (Jeremiah 6:16), because you were carrying something that could not fit through the door. God's doors can be large and lead us to new encounters of His presence or a new experience of healing and that is why these doors are never big enough for a poverty mindset, or unforgiveness, or unbelief. We are doors; and Psalm 24:7 says, "lift up your heads O ye gates and be lifted up ye everlasting doors and the king of glory will come in."

So, we can keep ourselves from moving forward along God's path.

It's not always our sins that we hold on to that keep us from passing through the door. It can be resistance, perhaps from an unseen evil. We have an enemy, remember. That is why, as ancient doors and gates, we must look up. This is where our light and release come from. God never keeps us from taking our heavenly steps. He wants us to be able to move freely and travel to where we need to be. It's ourselves, or satan's strategies, that get in the way. Look up and ask for help. Meditate on the words of wisdom God is speaking to us, revealing where we need a release or what we need victory over. He stands at the door and knocks. He bids us go through.

*Lord, we thank you that you are moving us. We will take one "heaven step" after the other until we reach our God-given destination. Amen.*

# WINNING AT LIFE

## ARE YOU OPPOSING GOD'S VICTORY IN YOUR LIFE?

C.S. Lewis once wrote, "there is no neutral ground in the universe, every square inch, every split-second is claimed by God and counter-claimed by satan." If we realize that this is the true battle which is constantly persisting until the end of this age, we will be reminded to be on guard and vigilant in reminding the enemy who we are. We are victors in Christ Jesus. Our prayers should be filled with proclamations of victory. This grants us assurance of triumph and reminds the enemy who we are in the battle. C.S. Lewis' quote provides a great definition for the spiritual battle that we are a part of every day. Time was created by God, and He isn't bound by it, but satan is. He only has so much time and he knows it. So, our prayers should confirm to us that in every moment and circumstance we are the winners—the victors in Jesus. The opposition to our victory is when we believe there is neutral ground, or we think we are only victorious in certain circumstances, but not all. Do not be deceived by some arbitrary line of demarcation. Stand and declare "I am the winner here, because in this moment I believe God, His Word, and what He has done for me." This is how we stop opposing our own victory: we declare the truth. Let's gain ground together and proclaim our King's victory.

> *Lord, we boldly confess that we are victors in Jesus and we are covered in His blood that delivered us from all sin, and even from death. Because of this, we declare Psalm 118:15 that "there will be the sound of joyful shouting and salvation in our tents because we are righteous and the right hand of the Lord fights for us and wins."*

*You have given us the shield of your salvation and your right hand upholds us and your gentleness makes us great. Psalm 18:35*

*Others May boast in chariots or horses but we will boast in the name of the Lord Our God. Others have bowed down and fallen but we have risen and stood upright. Psalm 27: 8*

*For all this and more, Lord, we thank you for giving us the victory through our Lord Jesus Christ. Amen*

## ARE YOUR PRAYERS IMPRESSIVE?

As we have been contemplating winning at life and living victoriously in Christ, it makes us think of what it means to be a winner. At one time or another, we have all been compelled by a winner. Does Jesus' life impress you? It should, because He is the ultimate Winner, the all-time champion of life. There isn't one person—past, present or future—who can say they won the battle with sin and death and overcame the grave, unless that person accomplished such a monumental feat by the will and power of God. The only person to ever do this is Jesus. I would say this is "Winning in Life"!

When we read about Jesus' life, hopefully we are impressed to follow Him, obeying His commands and giving Him honor; and in return He grants us the favor to become winners as we live our own lives. To live a "winning life" we need to pray impressive prayers, because we have an impressive God.

This is why praying Scriptures and speaking the Truth, is so vital to the victorious, miraculous life. The Scriptures are the ingredients to effective prayers.

Let's look at the definition of impress: to make someone feel adoration or respect. One day, Jesus will be adored and respected by all creation. Revelation 5:13 tells us:

> And every created thing which is in heaven and on the earth and under the earth and on the sea and all things in them, I heard saying, "to Him who sits on the throne, and the Lamb, be blessing and honor and glory forever and ever.

A second definition of impress is: make a mark using a stamp or seal.

> Ephesians 1:13NIV: And you also were included in Christ when you heard the message of Truth, the Gospel of your salvation. When you believed you were marked in him with a seal, the promised Holy Spirit.

# Prayers of Triumph

A third definition of impress is: fix an idea in one's mind.

1 Corinthians 2:16: Who has known the mind of Christ, the Lord so as to instruct Him, but we have the mind of Christ.

*Lord, we are in awe of you. Your goodness never ends. Your power is infinite and your love is never-ending. Your grace has no bounds and your victory is matchless. Because we adore you we will draw close, and as we draw near to you and you draw near to us, may our lives be a true impression of our Lord. Oh, that people will see we are marked and sealed with a promise—the Holy Spirit.*

*Lord, impress upon our minds victorious thoughts, that lead us to victorious prayers, that begin to shape a victorious life. Thank you, Lord, that you won the battle and we are victors and winners in you. May this truth be impressed upon us every day. In Jesus' name we believe and have the victory. Amen*

## THE SWEET SMELL OF VICTORY

Our prayers can produce fruit. Imagine the sweetest, choicest fruit emerging in the situations of your life; even in the most difficult situations or battles that you have faced. You can experience and express the sweetness of the Lord over your circumstances:

> Psalm 141:2 (ISV) …let my prayer be like incense offered before you and my uplifted hands like the evening sacrifice.

Our prayers that produce the fruit of God's victory are the ones that proclaim His might and power in our lives. David's Psalm 18 is one example.

> Psalm 18:16-19 (NKJV) He sent from above He took me: He drew me out of many waters. He delivered me from my strong enemy, from those two hated me. For they were too strong for me. They confronted me in the day of my calamity but the Lord was my support. He also brought me out into a broad place. He delivered me because He delighted in me.

Our God delights in us. As you pray and bring God delight, He will fight for you. He goes before you and tramples down the enemy, making a road: a highway in the desert or mountain place. So now you can pass, and as you do the sweet fragrance of victory will prevail over your circumstances and impact those you encounter, because you are a 2 Corinthians 2:14 victor:

> Now thanks be to God who always leads us in the triumph in Christ and through us diffuses the fragrance of his knowledge and every place. (NKJV)

Let's pray.

*Lord, we want to be carriers of your knowledge that brings forth a beautiful fragrance-the sweet smell of victory in you. As you lead us, may we be confident in your might and strength. May we walk in love, which never fails and always has the victory. Just as Christ loved us and gave himself for each of us, our offering and sacrifice to God is a fragrant aroma. As we follow after you, proclaiming your triumph over the enemy, sin, and death, may we enjoy the spoils of a war fought justly with fairness and righteousness.*

*As we attain this knowledge, may we truly know what it means to walk in victory everywhere we go, carrying the fragrance of the knowledge of our God. In Jesus' name we pray, amen.*

# WHAT SATAN DOESN'T WANT YOU TO KNOW

## DO YOU PRAY LIKE YOU KNOW GOD?

1 John 3:1 (NKJV): Be hold, what manner of love the Father has bestowed on us, that we should be called children of God! Therefore, the world does not know us, because it did not know Him.

The devil doesn't want us to know God's love fully. He wants to blind us to what it is like to be a true child of God; a child who knows their Father and remains in the truth at all times. Satan is the world's representative, and we are not of this world. So 1 John 3:1 tells us that satan cannot possibly know God, or us. He opposes God, because he wanted to be worshipped, and only God is worthy of worship. The devil knows that we worship God, but he doesn't understand the nature of God.

1 John 3:8 says that "he who sins is of the devil for the devil has sinned since the beginning." 1 John 3:6 makes it clear that those who sin do not know God.

The devil doesn't want you to know that he doesn't truly understand the character and power of God.

Too often, we think satan has a clear understanding of this, because he attacks, torments, lies, and pursues our destruction. He does this because he sees us as his enemy and threat, (which we are), but he doesn't know all that we are capable of! We become more capable the more we allow God to change us. Satan is only aware of those things that God has told him or shown him. God did not tolerate satan's rebellion for a moment, and although God allows him to run free for a little while, eventually he will be locked up for eternity.

The rest isn't clear just yet, because satan gets his orders from God. And satan is so far from the nature of God and

His righteousness that he cannot be fully aware of what that righteousness can hold; the glory of God is so far removed from the enemy that when he encounters it, he is done in every time. This is why we should be praying like children of God: full of love and full of His glory and righteousness. These prayers are prayers that can continue to prove to you, and to the enemy, that you are loved and adopted into the Kingdom—the Kingdom that satan doesn't understand and wants to destroy.

So, pray like you know God!

1 John 3 tells us that those who have been born of God do not sin. The more you live the life of rebirth, the more removed we become from the enemy's tactics, and the less he knows about us. Because as we move from darkness (the world) into light (the Kingdom), the less he understands our nature or power in Christ. Our prayers can literally cast satan far from us. As we speak the reality of Kingdom authority and God's Word, he has to flee. Righteous, effective prayers confound the enemy and remove him from our lives.

Let's pray like we know God; like we have been adopted like we intend to remove satan's proximity and his understanding.

*Heavenly Father, you are the Alpha and the Omega. You are the King who reigns over all the earth. You are the God that fully knows us and fully loves us. We praise you that this love, that sets us apart from the enemy, and your righteousness, that you impart to us when we become reborn, is so foreign to him that we become someone that he cannot understand. He no longer knows us because we are not of this world anymore.*

*Thank you that we are sanctified in you, which makes us far removed from our enemy. Lord, our intimacy with you separates us from sin, the world, and all our foes. We choose not to be in communion with the world; and as we turn aside to be with you, we become less and less familiar with the thoughts and actions of this world. This is where we want to be—unfamiliar to sin and known by our God; strangers in this world. We pray this in Jesus' name. Amen.*

## YOU ARE ALMOST THERE...

Satan doesn't want you to know right before you are on the verge of a breakthrough, he tries to send apathy, depression, weariness, distractions, or conflicting voices of advice against you to knock you off course. He doesn't want you to know that the more time you spend in the presence of God, being specific with your prayers; the more breakthrough and healing you receive. We try to pray ourselves out of messes and tests. Instead, we should invite the wisdom of God, the healing of Jesus, and the counsel of Holy Spirit into our lives and our situations. When God is ushered into our lives through true prayer and worship, circumstances change; they have to! God is divine, and He releases divinity into our lives. Jesus is truth and our healer, granting us freedom and restoration. Holy Spirit is our comforter and counselor, giving us wisdom and peace.

The entire 35th chapter of Isaiah talks about the future glory of Zion. Satan doesn't want you to know that this chapter applies to you and your life. If you remain in God, you will see the goodness of the Lord in the land of the living. So, whatever mess or test you are in, refuse to remain there by inviting, even urging, God to attend to you there. Don't be fooled into thinking that this prayer is always quick and easy. This is not to say that prayers can't be answered entirely on the basis of God's goodness or our foundational relationship with Him. But often, your prayer should be specific, contending for the end that you know your heavenly Father has for you. This isn't to imply that all situations require a pre-determined amount of prayer or fervency, but more often than not, God wants our time and attention, desiring our hearts and minds to be solely focused on Him and learning what He would like to do as we cooperate with Him.

Wouldn't you say this is how we build our relationship and lay the foundation for greater works? Isaiah 35 is a beautiful and powerful way to ask God to come into your situation, while telling satan he has to go, and letting him know that you figured out while *in* your mess or test that you are going to keep standing

# Prayers of Triumph

until the end—the end that God has decreed. Together, let's pray Isaiah 35 over our lives and over our mess, or test. This is how we fight the good fight. These words are alive and active, and they *will* produce fruit in our current situations no matter how difficult. Let these words soak in and saturate the test and trials.

Isaiah 35 is a powerful prayer that brings us hope for restoration.

> *Even the wilderness and desert will be glad in those days.*
> *The wasteland will rejoice and blossom*
> *with spring crocuses.*
> *Yes, there will be an abundance of flowers*
> > *and singing and joy!*
> *The deserts will become as green as the mountains*
> *of Lebanon,*
> > *as lovely as Mount Carmel or the plain of Sharon.*
> *There the* Lord *will display his glory,*
> > *the splendor of our God.*
> *With this news, strengthen those who have tired hands,*
> > *and encourage those who have weak knees.*
> *Say to those with fearful hearts,*
> > *"Be strong, and do not fear,*
> *for your God is coming to destroy your enemies.*
> > *He is coming to save you."*
>
> *And when he comes, he will open the eyes of the blind*
> > *and unplug the ears of the deaf.*
> *The lame will leap like a deer,*
> > *and those who cannot speak will sing for joy!*
> *Springs will gush forth in the wilderness,*
> > *and streams will water the wasteland.*
> *The parched ground will become a pool,*
> > *and springs of water will satisfy the thirsty land.*
> *Marsh grass and reeds and rushes will flourish*
> > *where desert jackals once lived.*
>
> *And a great road will go through that once deserted land.*
> > *It will be named the Highway of Holiness.*
> *Evil-minded people will never travel on it.*
> > *It will be only for those who walk in God's ways;*
> > *fools will never walk there.*

*Lions will not lurk along its course,*
>*nor any other ferocious beasts.*
*There will be no other dangers.*
>*Only the redeemed will walk on it.*
*Those who have been ransomed by the LORD will return.*
>*They will enter Jerusalem singing,*
>*crowned with everlasting joy.*
*Sorrow and mourning will disappear,*
>*and they will be filled with joy and gladness.*

## YOUR PRAYERS HAVE ETERNAL WEIGHT

Satan doesn't want you to know that you pray eternal prayers. He doesn't want you to know that time spent with the Holy Spirit can bring healing to every situation. Did you ever think that every problem, sin, bad habit, dilemma, and sickness can be brought to a place of repentance, peace, and ultimately healing, by allowing the Holy Spirit to counsel, minister, and comfort you? The Spirit of God is an unlimited force in our lives. If we pray eternal prayers we are inviting the Spirit to work in our lives and situations in a lasting way.

What is an eternal prayer? It's a prayer that has the present, earthly life in mind, and the future, eternal life in full view as well. We are eternal beings. 1 Corinthians 6:19 reminds us that our bodies are a temple of the Holy Spirit. He is eternal, so we carry eternity within us. When He counsels us, it transcends our earthly lives. Heaven, and eternity with our God and Father is the ultimate healing, so when we spend time with the counsel of the Holy Spirit, He speaks to us with eternal words. Eternal prayers are created and developed through time well-spent with the Holy Spirit. The enemy doesn't want you to know this because the Holy Spirit is our Source of help. He was sent by the Father in Jesus' name to teach us ALL things and bring to our remembrance ALL that Jesus has said to us. (John 14:26.)

Eternal prayers can be fulfilled on earth or in heaven. We are not here just to get a ticket "up" to heaven when we leave this earth, but we are being prepared for the Kingdom. 2 Timothy 2:12 tells us that if we endure hardship here, we will also reign with Him in eternity. When we pray we have to have faith that God is answering *how* and *when* as an eternal God. This is true because He loves us beyond this earthly life. We must trust Him because He not only sees us as we are, but as we will be.

*Lord, you are an eternal God that sees and knows everything. We praise you that you are all-knowing and you are not bound by time. What a gift we have in knowing that we can trust you to hear our prayers and* answer them in such a way that brings completeness and wholeness to our entire existence, not just the earthly vapor that we are living out now.

Help us, Lord, to go deeper in our prayer time—to capture all of you as the eternal God and King. Holy Spirit, remind us that we are larger than just this life. You are building us, completing us, for the Kingdom. Jesus, thank you. Amen.

# 5

# Prayers of *Goodness and Glory*

# ELECT GOODNESS

## PRAYERS THAT CAMPAIGN FOR THE WAY OF THE LORD

John the Baptist campaigned for Jesus. He told the people that He was coming and what He would do. John urged them to repent and be baptized. Mark 1:2-3 (NKJV):

> Behold, I send my messenger before your face, who will prepare your way before you. The voice of one crying out in the wilderness. "Prepare the way of the Lord: make his paths straight."

I don't think that God was saying that John was going to make Jesus' life and mission easier. God and Jesus both knew what He came to do and how He would need to do it. Making His paths straight perhaps meant giving Him room to reach you—to find you—to minister to you and to accomplish His Father's good work in you.

How were people to make a way? Mark 1:5 (NKJV) tells us,

> Then all the land of Judah and those from Jerusalem went out to him and were all baptized by him in the Jordan River, confessing their sins.

When we repent and ask forgiveness of sins it makes a way for God to reach us. Prayers that campaign for the way of the Lord are prayers of repentance. John was essentially telling them they needed to be free of themselves and their sins. He was saying they needed to be ready for Jesus so they could experience all that He had for them. They couldn't be sin-ridden and attain all that was to be manifested to them when they saw Jesus face-to-face.

We can pray prayers that campaign for the way of the Lord in our lives by confessing our sins. We hear that confession is good for the soul. Our souls need to be continually ministered to by the Holy Spirit. Our souls can cause us to hurt emotionally, physically, and spiritually. Our spirits are made alive to God upon salvation, but our souls can cause us trouble and separation from God.

There are many facets to effective prayer, but if you are praying for God to move heaven and earth or are contending for a breakthrough, don't you think you should begin with confession of your sins? Have you ever thought that when you confess and repent, demons run and flee? Think how many spiritual battles could be won with confession!

The word "campaign," when used as a noun, means a series of military operations intended to achieve a particular objective, confined to a particular area, or involving a specified type of fighting. Our prayers are how we fight. We fight in prayer, making a way for the Lord and then He goes before us and fights for us.

Let us pray.

*Lord, you are sovereign and only you can forgive our sins, transgressions, and iniquities. Search us, oh God, and know our hearts; try us and know our anxieties, and see if there is any wicked way in us. And lead us in the way everlasting (Psalm 139:23). Lord, as you are faithful to answer this prayer, we will confess; we will repent, and we will make a way for you. And as we do this, we will have the assurance that in so doing, we draw near to you and you to us. As you draw near to us the path is cleared and you, our Lord, go before us and fight for us. In Jesus' name. Amen.*

## PRAYERS THAT TELL OF HIS GOODNESS

When we pray, we often testify to God's goodness. We should also tell others about the good things He has done. We all have a general sense of God's goodness by simply experiencing His creation, His salvation, His provision, His mercy, and so much more. We read about His goodness in Scripture. But God wants us to know the depths of His goodness. I believe when we speak of God's goodness, His response is, "Yes, I am good; but I want you to know just how good." This is God talking about the details of our lives. We have a relational God. He goes beyond the God of the universe and becomes our personal God. Jesus becomes our personal Savior. Holy Spirit becomes our personal counselor, all the while doing the same for everyone else; hence, the God of the Universe. This is how it has to be. God knew He had to be personal with us, and He wants to be.

God is love. What is more personal than that? We discover just how good He is within our prayer life. The multitudes who don't seek God, who don't know Him, still experience His goodness as a byproduct of being part of His creation. The Word tells us over and over that God helps those who call out to Him or choose to go to Him.

Understanding and experiencing just how good He is requires us to move towards Him in humility, inviting Him into our lives in very specific ways, because He wants to work on the details. So why don't we give Him our biggest fears, our deepest hurts, our chronic pains, our life-long addictions. How wonderful it would be to let God's goodness eradicate these strongholds. These are the areas of our souls that need to know *just how good* He is.

But this requires some action on our part. We must do something.

> Psalm 34:8 (NIV): Taste and see that the Lord is good; how blessed is the man who takes refuge.

So, we must taste His goodness and we will be blessed.

Nahum 1:7 (NIV): The Lord is good, a refuge in times of trouble. He cares for those who trust in Him."

We need to make Him our Hiding Place.

Psalm 86:5 (NIV): For you, Lord, are good and ready to forgive and abundant in loving kindness to all who call upon you."

Here, all we have to do is call upon Him and we can receive forgiveness and love.

II Samuel 7:28 (NKJV): "And now, O Lord God, You are God, and Your words are true, and You have promised this goodness to Your servant."

Let's pray.

*God, you are love and your goodness flows because of it. Your goodness knows no bounds. It can bring us to repentance. Your goodness is enough to carry us through any circumstance. Your goodness is out of this world. Your goodness is our guide out of trouble, sickness, and sin; out of any mess that we may be in. Your goodness is the antidote for the human condition.*

*We want to know just how good you are. Today we give you the details of our lives. Those places that need an indwelling and revelation of just how good you are to us. So, we trust you with it all and we believe we will see the goodness of the Lord in the land of the living. (Psalm 27:13) In Jesus' name we pray. Amen.*

# THE GREATEST NAME

## LET HEAVEN AND NATURE SING— THE BIOLOGY OF PRAYER

The word "symbiotic" takes me back to Biology class. (It might do the same for you.) I liked biology in high school and college, but I *love* God's biology lessons.

Let's examine this biology lesson, for instance:

> Blessed is the man who trusts in the Lord, and whose hope is the Lord. For he shall be like a tree planted by the waters, Which spreads out its roots by the river, And will not fear when heat comes; But its leaf will be green, And will not be anxious in the year of drought, Nor will cease from yielding fruit (Jeremiah 17:7-8 NKJV).

This lesson tells us that, when our hope is in Jesus, we will be like a green, lush tree that always bears fruit. Jesus is our hope and our prayer as well. Don't we always pray in Jesus's name—the name above all names? The most powerful name? I have found myself declaring the name of Jesus over situations, meaning that my prayer is the name "Jesus." The greatest name *is* the prayer.

I want to share another biology lesson. It involves the Greatest Name Prayer and my cat, Gary. (It was only a matter of time before Gary became one of my prayer points.)

I started to pray this prayer over my cat. Yes, I really experienced the effectiveness and power of this prayer through my relationship with my cat. He *is* one of God's creatures. Gary lives in my backyard along with the oak, pine and maple trees, red-headed woodpeckers, squirrels, deer, foxes and blue jays, among other things. God created the heavens and the earth and all that's in it so we would be able to enjoy His glory of creation. When the heavens, nature, and God's creatures go about living out their existence, they respond to Him consistently and faithfully every time. They are affected by their environment, yet they don't change in attribute or integrity. I see this in my cat. He is pure and authentic in his creation. I have such a deep appreciation for him. Our relationship is symbiotic. We are different, but we benefit from one another. I actually see nature singing within him. I believe God has used Gary to show me His glory. What has God used within nature to show you His glory?

God intended for us to have a symbiotic relationship with His creation. These relationships are pure and simple, just as relationships should be. This pure relationship takes all the complication out of the equation. I believe that is why the Greatest Name Prayer was effective with my cat. I had been experiencing God's glory within Gary for a while, so when the vet said he would never walk on his hind leg, I brought him home and began praying the Greatest Name Prayer. I prayed for a miracle. I prayed "Jesus" over my cat, and I meant it, and Gary received it. I believe that's because of the simple relationship. He was completely healed in a few months and has been for years now. It was that powerful—and that simple.

What I learned from this is that when I am like the tree planted by the water, because I have put all my hope in the Lord, I am blessed in every way. And, it is evident, that even the creatures that live in my backyard receive the blessing as well!

*Lord Jesus, you are great and worthy to be praised. Your name is above all names. Thank you that the heavens and earth sing of your glory and they prove to us that there is a divine Creator who loves us. We have many gifts within your creation and as we live among them all, help us to see and experience your beauty. Thank you that you intended for us to be in relationship with all you created. Creation sings of your glory, helping us to declare your goodness and sovereignty. It helps us see that all we need is to call upon and believe in the Greatest Name; the name of Jesus. Amen.*

# FOCUS

## CAN YOU SEE THE HARVEST?

Let's combine two ideas to gain a clear picture of something the Lord is speaking about. The first is *focus,* which is our series title, and *harvest*. Harvest means the process of gathering crops.

Well, we don't have a crop unless we have done some planting, and we all have done some planting. Most of us have done this individually and collectively as a body of believers.

What does planting look like? It is praying, choosing righteousness, believing the truth, keeping the faith, standing on the Word, sharing the gospel, giving of our gifts and talents and time and tithes, and many other things that bring goodness and godliness to our lives and to those around us. God is saying we cannot forget what we have done in His name. Remember the planting and caring, and yes, the praying, because He is faithful to bring all the seed we have sown to fruition so that it can be harvested. Now is the time to focus on the harvest.

We have some gathering to do.

What is God showing you right now? What has God asked you to plant, water, and nurture that has not been harvested yet? Focus on those things during a time of prayer and fasting. God wants to show us what is ready to be harvested within us, our families, our churches, and our communities. What is the fruit of your godly labor? Be ready to see it, because the yield is just around the corner.

Focus on the fruit when you pray and fast, not on the seed.

At the time of planting, we sow small seed which does not resemble the fruit-bearing plant it will eventually become. That is why it is so important to focus on the fruit—the goodness of life.

God is speaking to many of His people, assuring us as churches, as families, and as individuals that the harvest is here for many prayers.

What did God plant in you? What did He ask you to plant? Well, it is ready. So, you must be ready as you pray and fast, and the <u>harvest will come into focus</u>.

> 2 Corinthians 9:10 (AMP): Now He who provides seed for the sower and bread for food will provide and multiply your seed for sowing, (that is your resources) and increase the harvest of your righteousness (which shows itself in acts of goodness, kindness and love.)
>
> 2 Corinthians 9:10 (TPT): This generous God who supplies abundant seed for the farmer, which becomes bread for our meals, is even more extravagant toward you. First, He supplies every need plus more. Then he multiplies the seed as you sow it, so that the harvest of your generosity will grow.

*Lord, you are the Master Gardener. The seeds are your seeds. All that we have planted and sown was first a desire of your heart. Thank you for asking us to be part of the plan and for asking us to plant. Because now we will enjoy the harvest with you. Just as a farmer sacrifices sleep and his or her own plans and wishes during the harvest season, help us to make the sacrifices necessary during this appointed time, so we can be sure the seed is harvested and produces an abundance of fruit. As your people, we are thankful for your supply. We are expectant, in this time, to see how our fruit is going to meet the demands of those who need it. Jeremiah 17:10 tells us that you search the heart and test the mind, and you give to us according to our ways, according to the fruit of our doings.*

*So, Lord, remind us of what we have planted. Help us to see it by our commitment to prayer and fasting, and we will surely focus our eyes where you direct us. In Jesus' name. Amen.*

## PRAYERS THAT KEEP YOU FIXED

Today's world moves quickly. We are living in an age of acceleration. As we near the end of this age, we see tremendous acceleration of information throughout the earth. Think about the Kingdom information that still needs to be imparted to God's people. Therefore, God is sending revelation quickly. But we can still remain joyous, centered, and focused people if we keep our eyes fixed on the Lord and look full in His wonderful face.

Peter looked into His wonderful face.

If we don't keep Jesus as our focus, we can get off course, like Peter. When he had his eyes on Jesus, he was able to walk on the water, but when he looked at the wind and the waves he began to sink.

If we don't keep our eyes fixed or focused on Jesus, we will fall.

We are always in motion. Even as we sleep and are at rest, our bodies are working. They remain active, restoring and regenerating for the next day. Since we are always in motion, it is essential to the Christian walk to keep our eyes fixed on Jesus.

An ice skater, in full spin, moves at a rate of 308 to 500 revolutions per minute. It is crucial for the skater to fix their eyes on an object and find it within every revolution. If that does not occur, the skater will become dizzy and sick, and will most likely fall. Their eyes can even temporarily develop nystagmus–a condition of the eye where rapid movement up and down or right to left may occur. This condition can even cause loss of vision. It seems like it is easy to get out of focus and lose our vision of God, and His plan, in this busy, sensory-overloaded world. So, together, let's find our divine object—our heavenly King of kings and keep our eyes fixed on Jesus, so we can stay the course and remain standing on His promises.

> John 14:12-14 (NIV): "Very truly I tell you, whoever believes in me will do the works I have been doing, and they will do even greater things than these, because I am going to the Father. And I will do whatever you ask in my

name, so that the Father may be glorified in the Son. You may ask me for anything in my name, and I will do it."

Jesus went to His Father. He is seated at the right hand of God the Father. The throne of God needs to be our focus; Jesus operates from this place. He answers prayers in His name from this very location.

Hebrews 12:2 (NIV): Fixing our eyes on Jesus, the pioneer and perfecter of faith. For the joy set before Him He endured the cross, scorning its shame, and sat down at the right hand of the throne of God.

Again, we see He is seated at the right hand of the throne of God. Let's go to prayer and focus on Jesus—God's "Right-Hand Man."

*Jesus, you are more beautiful and worthy of our gaze than anything in this world. You are the only reason we are able to stand in such a time as this. Where else should we look? Jesus, you are all we need to remain upright, on our feet, strong and steady, and centered for our walk and witness. Wherever you may call us, we will be able to go because you are our guide. Let us remain with eyes fixed upon you and then your goodness and love will come into full view, fueling us for the journey. In your name we pray. Amen.*

<u>Turn Your Eyes Upon Jesus</u>
O soul, are you weary and troubled?
No light in the darkness you see?
There's a light for a look at the Savior
and life more abundant and free.

So, turn your eyes upon Jesus,
look full in His wonderful face,
and the things of earth will grow strangely dim.
In the light of His glory and grace.
(Helen Howarth Lemmel, public domain)

## WHEN YOU PRAY DO YOU FOCUS YOUR HOPE ON YOUR PRAYER, OR YOUR GOD?

You might be focusing on your prayer if:

When your prayers don't get answered, or answers are delayed, or maybe people aren't cooperating with you, you get upset, discouraged, or maybe bitter.

I'm learning that if my prayers are truly focused on my hope and belief in God, then I don't find myself upset when things don't go according to my prayers.

Think about it. We pray to God because we know what He is capable of. He has capabilities that shape worlds with His words. We don't pray to ourselves, but we rely too quickly on our own prayers. Instead, we need to rely on *Him*!

This isn't to say we don't honestly and openly share our emotions with our Father, because that is one of the gifts of our relationship with Him. But, too often we determine within ourselves what the outcome should look like, then we pray accordingly, and become discouraged when our scenario doesn't play out.

So, if we focus on our God and His wonder-working abilities, and less on what we prayed, our hope and belief will grow and we will begin to receive. This is because we are no longer focused on a limited prayer, but on an unlimited God.

Prayer:

*Romans 16:27 (NASB): To the only wise God, through Jesus Christ, be the glory forever.*
*Psalm 147:5: Lord, you are abundant in strength and your understanding is infinite.*

*There is no one like you. That is why we come to you in earnest prayer. Forgive us for thinking we know the end, or the answer; only you are the Alpha and Omega. We give you our prayers and ask that you shape and mold them to be an offering to you, and effective to bring cooperation with you and the Holy Spirit to accomplish your good works.*

*You made the whole earth by your power. You established the world in your wisdom and by your understanding you stretched out the heavens. (Jeremiah 10:12)*

*Today we recommit some prayers to you. Help us to pray according to your will. May you teach us how to pray powerful, righteous, holy, and glory-filled prayers. In Jesus' name. Amen.*

# GLORY

## IT'S BEST TO PRAY YOUR WORRIES AWAY

In Matthew 6:25-34 Jesus tells us not to worry about what we need: what we will eat, what we will wear, or the troubles of tomorrow. He was telling the disciples not to worry, because it makes it impossible for God to bring all that He has to us. Our relationship is a partnership. He waits on us for our contribution, which is usually a surrendered will to Him.

> Matthew 6: 33-34 (KJV): "But seek ye first the kingdom of God, and His righteousness; and all these things shall be added unto you. Take therefore no thought for the morrow: for the morrow shall take thought for the things of itself. Sufficient unto the day is the evil thereof."

What is God trying to add to you?

Let's think about our prayer lives for a minute.

We usually do one of the following:

Pray about our needs and wants incessantly or pray about them with our own understanding.

Worry about our needs and wants and forget to pray.

Pray about our needs and wants and then go back to worrying about them.

We can't pray anymore double-minded prayers.

Matthew 6 tells us to seek the kingdom first and all the necessities will be added to us. God wants to add increase to your life. Is your life lacking something? God wants to add a blessing, a provision, a promise to you. But, are you too busy telling Him what to do? Our prayers are meant to be Kingdom prayers.

Let's pray a Kingdom prayer together.

*Lord, what are you doing today?*

*You are eternally magnificent and glorious, so tell us what you are doing through your glory this day. We want to be a part of it. May that glory shine upon us and burn away our thoughts, and leave only a brilliant residue of your glory so we can filter our day through it. You know what we need more than we do. Show us where to focus our minds, our intentions, and our hands so you can advance the Kingdom today as you guide us. Show us what you want to add to us, and may we have eyes to see it. Increase the areas that are deficient within us.*

*Matthew 6 says not to worry about what we will wear; so clothe us in peace. You tell us not to worry about what we will eat; so may we taste and see that you are good. You remind us to focus on the present day; tomorrow will worry about itself, so help our souls to be steadfast and set upon you. We thank you for your patience with us as we learn how to receive what you have for us. In Jesus' name we pray. Amen.*

## Prayers of Goodness and Glory

**YOUR PRAYERS DON'T HAVE TO BE DULL.**

Some say Psalm 24 was written by David after he obtained the Ark of the Covenant and was returning it to Jerusalem, so that it would abide in the temple. When we read this passage, most of us are drawn to verses 7 and 9:

> Lift up your heads O ye gates and be lifted up you everlasting doors.

Some theologians believe these verses were speaking literally to the temple, as it was about to receive the glory of the Lord and become its dwelling place. Others believe these verses are/were speaking to those who wanted to receive God's glory. It is believed that it's repeated because people needed to be reminded again of the seriousness of the weight of God's glory. God's glory brings a heavenly light to our lives and to our prayers.[1]

Do you feel dull anywhere? Are your prayers lackluster at times? His glory will turn our prayers into bright, sharp, lively prayers. We know when our prayers are full of His glory—they are crisp and sharp, bringing revelation to the situation. Have you ever prayed a prayer or spoken a word that edified you or someone else; a prayer that brought hope and a glimmer of God's goodness and presence? Well, that is a glory-filled prayer. The more of God's glory we receive, the more glorious our prayers will become. That's why we will stand together and let the declaration of Psalm 24 usher in His glory as we lift and open the doors of our churches and lift and open the gates of our souls.

> *The earth is the Lord's, and everything in it;*
> *the world, and all who live in it;*
> *for he founded it on the seas and established it on the waters.*
> *Who may ascend the mountain of the Lord?*
> *Who may stand in his holy place?*
> *The one who has clean hands and a pure heart,*
> *who does not trust in an idol or swear by a false god. They will*
> *receive blessing from the Lord*
> *and vindication from God their Savior.*

*Such is the generation of those who seek him*
*who seek your face, God of Jacob.*
*Lift up your heads, you gates;*
*be lifted up, you ancient doors,*
*that the King of glory may come in.*
*Who is this King of glory?*
*The Lord strong and mighty,*
*the Lord mighty in battle.*
*Lift up your heads, you gates;*
*lift them up, you ancient doors,*
*that the King of glory may come in.*
*Who is he, this King of glory?*
*The Lord Almighty—He is the King of glory.*

*Hallelujah!*

# EVERLASTING HOPE

### (New Hope Church has its first Sunday worship in a new location)

After many months of planning and hard work, New Hope Church has moved to a new location. We are blessed to be here and grateful for God's provision. We have taken hope with us, but this move has brought about even more hope, more faith and more expectation for what God is doing for us and within our church family.

We are in a place of New Hope. New-found hope has a new place. We are making room for New Hope.

We are going to be finding hope wherever we look; wherever we go. We will behold the mystery of Christ in us, the hope of glory.

> Colossians 1:26-27 (KJV): The mystery that has been kept hidden for ages and generations, but is now disclosed to the Lord's people. To them God has chosen to make known among the Gentiles the glorious riches of this mystery, which is Christ in you, the hope of glory.

What Paul is talking about here, and in verse 25, is the Word of God and its fullness. In John chapter one, John refers to Jesus as the Word. If we think about this verse in relation to Colossians 1:25, fullness of the Word could also be the fullness of the revelation of Jesus. So, Jesus and his fullness would be Christ in us—the hope of glory.

Jesus brought glory to God by living a sinless life of divine example and then by dying a cruel and painful, undeserving death. But that wasn't the end of His glory-giving to His Father, because He came to overcome death, and that is why His resurrection brought full glory to God. Christ in us gives us hope of an eternal glory. But while we are on earth, we must also consider the earthly life that Jesus lived, and how He glorified His father while living in a broken world. That is why, after studying this passage, we realize that the glory we look to in the coming age helps us to move from glory to glory while we too are here in a broken world.

Realizing the full glory of Jesus:
He was from the beginning.
He came to earth as a man.
He died and rose again.
He ascended into heaven.

This is what makes hope possible for us. This is also why we can experience contradictions in the Christian life, such as living and dying (to die is gain—Phillipians 1:21), and still realize that we move from glory to glory with triumph and victory. We have been filled with hope and joy, but we also experience momentary, earthly defeat, hardship, and sometimes pain and loss. But, yet we hope, because God has the final say. The full glory for us is yet to come.

> 2 Corinthians 3:18 (KJV): But we all, with open face beholding as in a glass the glory of the Lord, are changed into the same image from glory to glory, even as by the spirit of the Lord.

As we live, and are changed from glory to glory, our prayers become the vehicle to take us onward and upward. Our lives are a series of opportunities to find new hope in every situation. This is possible when we have Christ in us, our hope of glory.

Are you praying from a place of hope?

Do you need some new-found hope?

Knowing that the full glory for us to behold is yet to come- this can even fuel us when we are running on empty—or close to it.

Let us stand in a place of new hope and declare Christ is our hope of glory.

*Dear Lord, you are worthy to be praised. We glorify your name, your goodness, and your your sovereignty over us. Breathe your life-giving Spirit into us, and may we receive you, especially in the areas that need a revival of hope; a bigger glimpse of your glory.*

*We're thankful in all things. We are thankful that we share in Christ's glory but also in His sufferings. Because without His suffering there would be no true triumph and victory, which brings the fullness of Christ and releases hope to every situation. We thank you, Father, for your Son, our Savior. We know that it is Him in us; the hope of glory. Amen.*

## ENDNOTES

1  https://enduringword.com/bible-commentary/psalm-24/

# 6

# Prayers of Treasure

# RICHES

## A TREASURY OF PRAYER

Deuteronomy 26:18 (NIV): "And the Lord has declared this day that you are His people, His treasured possession as He promised, and that you are to keep all His commands."

When we pray, God is hearing His beloved—His treasures—speaking and calling out to Him. We must have confidence that we are loved and are a coveted possession of the Lord's; we are His workmanship. If we truly believe that we are His workmanship, than we must also believe He is always looking at us and seeing our full potential. He sees His final, perfect work of art that is us. We must keep in mind that our lives, and all that is within them, are to bring about His beauty and display His full creative power.

This demands a response from us; a response of rich prayers. Praying unearths the treasures not only within our lives, but also displayed through our lives. Have you ever prayed for someone else, and God used it to dig up and uncover treasures within you? Prayer brings about a richness of relationship with us and others. Have you ever spent time in intimate prayer and come away saying, "God, how did I not know that about you already"? Prayer brings about a richness of relationship with us and our Father, because God uncovers truth when we pray. Prayer is like a divine excavation, revealing what is hidden below.

God has placed eternity within us, which has deposited a treasury of prayers inside us.

God made us rich in Him. We were born wealthy. Our life of prayer can either speak to His goodness and authority, which are rich prayers—prayers that remind us we are co-heirs with Christ–or our prayers can become ineffectual, spoken from a mindset of poverty; prayers that are lacking faith in the God who richly supplies.

But, Philippians 4:19 (NIV) reminds us that God took care of it all.

> And my God He will meet all your needs according to the riches of His glory in Christ Jesus.

*Lord, you are good to us. We are in a place of abundance all the time. Your riches never run out. Your well of provision is always full. May our prayers be spoken truthfully, from a place of faith that our heavenly Father is the only supply we need. Thank you that we don't have to lack for anything. Lord, today we ask that we would make a withdrawal from your heavenly treasury, and we ask as your sons and daughters that you would enlighten us in a way that we have a better understanding of your heavenly resources. We want to know how to pray effective prayers that are rich in truth and power in Christ Jesus. It is in His name that we pray. Amen.*

## PRAYERS OF FELLOWSHIP

The most important relationship we can have is with Jesus. We hear this all the time, and we know it is fundamentally true of the Christian walk.

But what are we really doing about it?

Hopefully, spending time in the Word and praying. Our relationship with Jesus is like no other, because it brings all we need to our lives. Relationship with Jesus grants us a life of flourishing: eternal life, the abundant life, the peaceful life, the gift-bearing life, the fruit-bearing life, the successful life, the contented life, the joyful life, the hopeful life; the *rich* life.

This kind of life is acquired through spending time with Jesus in prayer. Most of us have come to realize the essential thing of this life is our walk with God, and how it affects us and our fellowship with others. In I John 1:1-7, John is simply telling us that Jesus came to earth, the disciples had a face-to-face experience with Him, and this became a point of fellowship among them; and so, even unto us. He goes on to say that to have true fellowship involving rich relationships, we have to walk in the light. This speaks to our righteousness in Him. We must be continually reminded of what it means to walk in the light.

Prayer keeps us in the light. We have relationship with God and others through honest communication. So, our prayer life draws us closer to God and others. This is true because when we come away from our prayer time we are changed: sins are confessed, revelation takes place, and we pray for others. All of this draws us close to our Lord and one another. Have you noticed that when you pray for someone you feel closer to them? Prayer is powerful and essential to rich relationships.

(Have you ever considered that maybe, for a season, you should spend more time with Jesus in prayer to work out a difficult relationship than trying to spend time with him/her? I am sure a closeness will develop.)

Jesus is the relationship mender. When we spend time in friendship with Jesus, we become more like Him, more authentic and better-equipped to create rich relationships.

Let's pray.

*God, you are jealous for us. We thank you for sending Jesus to mend our relationship with you—to make it possible to be worthy to come to you through Him. We thank you that the veil was torn and we can enter into an intimate and open New Testament relationship with you and others. One of the greatest gifts we have on this earth is sharing together in the revelation of who Jesus is. This glorious unveiling eternally bonds us as the body.*

*We thank you that iron sharpens iron, and we exhort and encourage each other into greater godliness and humility. We are family, and when one of us falls we have someone to help us back up. May our prayer lives usher us into the light of rich fellowship. Amen.*

## RICH FAITH REQUIRES LISTENING

Hearing is sometimes passive. *Listening* is active and intentional.

I have found, when I'm lacking in faith about something, it's because I haven't listened. I haven't allowed God to really speak to me. I have only heard Him.

Prayer is two-way communication.

Prayer takes communicating with our words and thoughts, but it also involves listening. Sometimes listening is downright difficult. Listening is willfull. You wait. Sometimes, waiting requires us to be still, other times it does not. God may ask us to do things in the waiting. Listening requires us to tune our ears and hearts to a posture of expectancy; where we know something is going to be shared. When you listen, you don't just hear someone out. Listening requires effort because the listener genuinely cares about what is being said. The listener knows it is vital to their situation, whatever that may be, and values the input of the speaker.

Have you ever been lost (obviously, before GPS were in every car or phone and you had to ask for directions)? You didn't just hear the person giving guidance. You listened. You repeated the instructions to yourself. Maybe you repeated them back to the person. You repeated them to the person in the car with you for confirmation. Sometimes you even wrote them down, or drew a diagram.

We need to do this with what God tells us in prayer. When we are listening for God's answers, for His voice to speak to us, we are exercising our faith. Sometimes answers come right away. Other times our faith is tested and we must wait. We become good listeners in the waiting, and we grow in the richness of our faith.

*Lord, you are faithful to us and we want to be faithful to you. We can trust you. We want you to be able to trust us. We all have a measure of faith, but we want to make that faith richer: as rich as it can be. We take the prayers that are between you and us and we purpose today to truly listen to what you are saying to us about those prayers. If we listen attentively, we are confident that you will speak even if it's not the answer we want.*

*All we truly need is a word from you—a word that gives us staying power to keep the faith and see it through. And those prayers that remain unanswered, we declare this day that we live by faith and not by sight (Hebrews 11:1). So, we will begin to listen with expectancy. We will wait in hope because we have rich faith. In Jesus' name we pray. Amen.*

# BREAKTHROUGH

## THE HOLY SPIRIT WILL LEAD OUR PRAYER LIVES IF WE LET HIM

Zechariah 4:6 (NASB): "...not by might nor by power, but by my spirit says the Lord of hosts."

We need to open our hearts to the Spirit. If we genuinely do this, our prayers will change. They will grow in stature. They may grow so big that they begin to break things that need to be broken! Your prayers will have more meaning to you and to those you are praying for, because they will be more effective, more righteous, and more insightful.

I John 4:13 (NIV): This is how we know that we live in Him and He in us. He has given us of His Spirit.

If we live in Him, we pray in Him.

"He has given us of His Spirit." If we believe this (and we do), our prayers can only come alive with the Spirit. If our prayers are Spirit-filled they will be powerful. The Word tells us the Holy Spirit has power. The Holy Spirit's power is endless. Therefore, we can overflow with hope knowing we have an endless supply of power available to us.

Romans 15:13 (NIV): May the God of hope fill you with all joy and peace as you trust in Him, so that you may overflow with hope by the power of the Holy Spirit.

Our prayers are so much better with hope.

Imagine approaching your prayers from a posture of abundant hope. That stance changes things, doesn't it?

> II Timothy 1:7 (NIV): For the spirit God gave us does not make us timid, but gives us power, love and self-discipline.

Again, we are told that the Spirit has the ability to bring power, God's power, into our lives; specifically, our prayer lives. The Spirit not only has power but He produces fruit. When we experience breakthrough, it's due to the fruit of prayer.

Galatians 5:22-23 is our prayer today. As we pray this Scripture, allow the Holy Spirit to speak to you about the situations you are currently praying about; those situations where you need a breakthrough. Together, let's believe in the power of the Spirit that helps us to be bold and hopeful in prayer, and to believe that by the power of the Spirit the fruits of the Spirit will be evident in our situations.

> But the fruit of the spirit is LOVE, JOY, PEACE, LONG-SUFFERING, KINDNESS, GOODNESS, FAITHFULNESS, GENTLENESS, SELF-CONTROL. Against such things there is no law.

*Lord, whatever we need to break through these things in our lives that are not right, we ask for it now in Jesus' name. We invite the fruit of the Spirit into each situation. Therefore, we need a greater revelation of the Spirit because all these things are brought to us by the Spirit. There is no law against such things. This means there are no bounds to what your Spirit and His power, and fruit, can do in each one of our lives. Amen.*

## LET GO

Are you praying like you need to let something go? Letting go of pain, fear, indifference, jealousy; letting go of self-will and surrendering to God.

Are you dying to what is alive in your flesh, so your spirit can come alive with what is lovely, true and pure?

Fleshly death hurts for a time, but the benefits far outweigh the momentary pain of letting go. It's kind of silly, not to mention sinful, to hold on to what is bad. Evil desires or self-centeredness are contrary to God's plan. Just because something is comfortable or makes sense to us doesn't mean it is good for us.

"Breakthrough deaths" can happen every day. They should be happening within us. Our example is Jesus, and we need to surrender like He did. Jesus made it clear that He only said what the Father told Him to say and He only did what the Father told Him to do. His Father told Him to surrender unto death, for love's sake. So, if you aren't able to surrender things like: TV, gossip, lust, fear, etc... the answer is to pray! Get close to God in your prayers. You may feel like Jesus did when He asked God why He had forsaken Him. But, God had an ultimate plan, for love's sake, that had to be fulfilled.

Last year on Easter, God spoke to me about miracles in the dark, and He told me that the greatest miracle of all time took place in the dark—in the darkness of a tomb, no doubt. Jesus had to surrender to make it to the tomb; to make it to the place of the greatest miracle. He had to die a *breakthrough death* to bring eternal life to all of mankind. So, you must pray and ask God to guide you and help you to surrender and give up some things, so you can die a few deaths unto yourself, and unto some worldly desires. This is how you experience breakthrough.

Prayer:

*Dear God, thank you for sending your Son, our wonderful Savior. Thank you Jesus for your surrender, which made it possible for us to celebrate the ultimate breakthrough, the miracle in the dark that overcame death and sin for all time.*

*Today we celebrate resurrection power in our lives by recognizing that we must surrender, like Jesus, and die to some things in our lives and within ourselves, in order to live fully within the resurrection power. We believe that as we give up worldly desires, it will become easier to live the "resurrection reality" wherein we only want to do and say what the Father would show us. Jesus, you have secured the ultimate victory, and for that today we praise you, honor you, and surrender to you. Amen.*

## WHAT ARE THE DIMENSIONS OF YOUR PRAYERS?

Isaiah 54:2-3 (NKJV):
Enlarge the place of your tent,
And let them stretch out the curtains of your dwellings;
Do not spare;
Lengthen your cords,
And strengthen your stakes.
For you shall expand to the right and to the left,
And your descendants will inherit the nations,
And make the desolate cities inhabited.

God's powerful Word and our faithful prayers can bring a stretching to our lives, a stretching that moves borders and makes room for a move of God. Most often we see in the Word that God asks us to make a move and then He causes big, wonderful things to happen; like cities being taken over, nations being saved from destruction, dry bones coming to life, the promised Messiah being born in safety, and ordinary men becoming rulers alongside kings. God is calling us to enlarge where we dwell. We can think and live bigger, because He is telling us to. Our prayers and bold declarations are the instruments of expansion.

This brings us to the next few verses of Isaiah 54:4-5:

> Do not fear, for you will not be ashamed;
> neither be disgraced, for you will not be put to shame;
> For you will forget the shame of your youth,
> And will not remember the reproach of your
>   widowhood anymore.
> For your Maker is your husband,
> The Lord of hosts is His name;
> And your Redeemer is the Holy One of Israel;
> He is called the God of the whole earth.

This is key to breaking through the doors that keep us out of the areas or dimensions that God wants to move us into. We can go boldly if we remember what He has promised us, so we need to put our past behind us and reach for, and step into, the places that are beyond our current capacity. We are landowners in the kingdom of God. Let's begin to take the land, and possess the land, together in prayer.

*Lord, we are in awe of you. You have wonderful things in store for us. We can live beyond what we realize. You are a breakthrough God. You break through time and space and the dimensions of heaven and earth. This is because you are the God of all. So, this reminds our hearts and minds that you are sovereign, and you still will be, in the places you are calling us to dwell. So, as we lengthen our cords and strengthen our stakes into the new areas and dimensions of our lives that you have ordered, we will do so boldly and with confidence, because your promises are for us and our descendants.*

*Lord, we thank you that you are bringing new hope into many areas of our lives. We are a people who are on the move and we are ready to go where your Spirit leads us. We declare that as we pray, read your Word, and follow the Holy Spirit's guiding, it will cause an expansion in our lives and in our faith. In Jesus' name we pray. Amen.*

## YOU ARE BREAKING THROUGH

God wants to encourage you right where you are; right where you are standing in prayer.

Some of you are standing in a hard place. But be encouraged that your prayers have been heard.

Be encouraged because we know if we stand faithfully in a place long enough, what is beneath us begins to break *down* and then we will break *through*. Be encouraged, and continue to stand on the promises, stand on the truth, stand on the Word, stand in faith, and today, God says to stand encouraged because He hears your prayers. We will begin to see these things that we are believing for break up through the ground; right where we are standing. Sometimes we get a breakthrough that is quick and earth-shattering, like glass breaking, but other times we break through by a consistent pressure.

Many of you are standing, you are praying, and you are believing, but you need some encouragement—a light for the next step. God is telling you to be of good cheer because He is a God that rewards those who believe and pray. So, it may not feel like things are shifting or breaking, but this could be a time where the ground below you—where you are standing—is moving one particle at a time. God says suddenly it will break wide open from the pressure of the press of your prayers. Satan may be trying to whittle you down, but you are whittling right back. The key to victory, to breakthrough, is to remember you already have the victory and there is no better advantage than that.

So again, God is saying, "It is simple. Be encouraged. Stand and keep standing in the press of prayer."

*Lord, we give you glory. You are a breakthrough God. You're able to break every yoke in our lives and in the lives of those we love. We want to capture the promise of Isaiah 35:4 (NIV):*

> *...say to those with fearful hearts,*
> *"Be strong, do not fear;*
> *your God will come,*

*He will come with vengeance;*
*with divine retribution*
*He will come to save you."*

And knowing this and receiving this as truth, as our promise to us today, we can stand and put on the armor again and again, as often as it takes. In Jesus' name we pray. Amen.

# TAILSPIN

## CENTRIC PRAYERS

We can get caught up in a tailspin often; maybe every day, or many times a day.

When a plane finds itself in a tailspin, it needs centering, which is done by the steering of the rudders, which must be applied in the opposite direction of the plane's direction of travel

Doesn't this sound like a spiritual analogy?

Our prayers can center us when we are tossed to and fro. Usually, our tailspin begins in our mind.

Isaiah 26:3 tells us that we "will keep in perfect peace if our mind is stayed and steadfast on God". This is a result of our trust in Him. Verse four goes on to say that we should trust in the Lord forever, because in Him is everlasting strength. We all have been weary of the battle—the tailspin in our thoughts. But we are to be steadfast, focused on Him, because He is one with everlasting strength, not us. Paul told the Romans how to do this in Romans 12:21. He writes, "do not be overcome by evil but overcome evil with good."

This is applying the rudders in the opposite direction.

Let's pray and believe in God's goodness.

*Lord, you are mighty and strong forever. You have enough strength for this life and the next. We are so thankful and grateful to you that you have the answers to keep us centered. You are the driving force in our lives. Holy Spirit, we ask that you show us how to overcome evil with good, so that not just in our inward life, but our outward expressions, you living strong in us, will be displayed.*

*We want to be centered and focused on your strength so we won't be thrown off course. We overcome evil with your goodness in our minds, our bodies, our relationships, our careers and ministries, our families, and our communities. We send forth your goodness to overcome any evil influence*

*that is present in our lives. We will be steadfast in our thoughts. Help us Lord. In Jesus' name we pray. Amen.*

## PRAY STEADY

Stay level as God moves you forward because He *is* the one relocating us. He is never still; only His voice is. He is always working on our behalf and He never sleeps. If you remember He's actively pursuing a good end to your situation, you will not get caught in a tailspin.

It's easier to stay ahead of a tailspin then to get out of one.

Stay in step with your Captain, the Divine Pilot, and you will avoid spinning out of control in your thoughts, and in your emotions, and along your journey.

How do you do this? In your prayer life. Your prayer life is your ticket to absolute altitude.

As we have seen throughout this book, there's nothing more effective than praying the Word; so let's do that together:

*Lord, you are always working on our behalf.*

> *John 5:17 (NKJV): But Jesus answered them, "My Father has been working until now, and I have been working."*

*You have our best interest in mind-always.*

> *John 3:17 (NKJV): Jesus answered and said to him, "What I am doing you do not understand now, but you will know after this."*

*We can and should trust you always.*

> *John 14:1 (NKJV): "Let not your heart be troubled; you believe in God, believe also in Me."*

*You save us from all of our troubles when we call upon You.*

> *Psalm 34:6 (NKJV):*
> *This poor man cried out,*
> *and the Lord heard him,*
> *And saved him out of all his troubles.*

*Again, Lord you are working in us and we should take comfort and confidence in this.*

*Phillipians 2:13 (NKJV): For it is God who works in you both to will and to do for His good pleasure.*

*Thank you that we can remain steady in your promises. Amen.*

# 7

# Prayers that *Make a Way*

# THE DOOR

### OPEN UP

Your relationship with Jesus opens doors for you. But first, we must open up to Him.

> Revelation 3:20 (TPT): "Behold, I'm standing at the door, knocking. If your heart is open to hear my voice and you open the door within, I will come in to you and feast with you, and you will feast with me."

Behold. Jesus is telling us "Take notice of me, not because I'm great (even though He is), but because I can and want to do great things for you. But you must allow me entrance so we may feast together."

How do we begin to behold Him? Ask God, "How do I behold your Son? How do you want me to see Him?"

Ask your Savior, "How do you want me to perceive you? How do you want me to see you?"

Ask the Holy Spirit, "Help me do this. Help me open my heart—the door within—so that I can hear Jesus' voice."

This is opening up the way for Jesus to enter—to enter into you. This is the door to relationship. There is no more intimate relationship that we can experience. This is why our prayers get answered in a unique fashion, differently from the way God might answer other people; why we hear different things when God speaks to us; and why we might be asked to do things that others may not be asked. When we open the door, we open it to our Personal Savior. He is so very capable and expert at loving us all the same, but also personally, in exactly the way each one of us needs. Don't you want to meet Him at the door every day in prayer?

He is waiting.

*Lord, Jesus, we are grateful to you for your perfect love towards us. It amazes us that you want to feast with us. Whether we are inviting you in at the door of salvation, or the door of healing, or the door of faith, since there are many doors, we want to be sure to swing our door wide so that everything you are is welcome to enter. Forgive us for the times we turned you away or only let a portion of you inside. We ask for wisdom, and turn to you, our Savior and our friend. We invite you into every area.*

*Holy Spirit, search our hearts and show us specifically where we have not welcomed you, and grant us wisdom and grace to receive: to behold Jesus and let Him be who and what we need in this area. Jesus, we long for a full spirit, a full heart, a full life—one that is in continual feast with you, your truth, and your Word, so that our stomachs may be full of your goodness. Thank you that you desire to come in and dine with us. Amen.*

## (DOOR) FRAMES: SOMETIMES WE NEED A PICTURE TO UNDERSTAND

What if your current difficulties were future open doors?

They are. God will turn these circumstances into opportunities. How do we begin to make a way, or construct an entrance for Him to enter? I believe sometimes we must begin to see with the eyes of our hearts. We need to see the bigger picture. When we examine what God has said with the eyes of our heart, it expands the place in us that can receive His promise. Ezekiel, starting in chapter 40, speaks of the new temple. It gives all the dimensions and design plans. I am amazed with the detail.

One thing you will notice is God's attention to the measurements of every aspect of the building, including the doorways.

We are the temple, and God will expand the place in us where He dwells through difficulties. The latter part of Ezekiel provides a picture for what we can't see, but usually feel, when God is reconstructing us.

*Lord, thank you that you want a larger space within us; an expansion of you on the inside. Thank you that you dwell within each of us. Thank you for circumstances that you are changing as we follow you. Help us see that you are growing us through each difficulty; they are an opportunity for you to reconstruct us. Help us see with the eyes of our heart what you are doing.*

*Can we fathom the mysteries of God? Can we know the limits of the Almighty? They are higher than the heavens and deeper than the depths. What can we do? What can we know? Their measure is longer than the earth and wider than the sea. (Job 11:7-9)*

*So, Lord have your way.*

## THE FUTURE

When we walk into a building, such as a hospital or shopping center, we have to pay attention to signage to make sure we get where we need to go. We walk through doors and hallways and then more doors. Often we must turn this way and that. There are usually a few ways to get to our destination, but there is always a best route.

Our futures are like this. We will get there, but *how* is the question. Just like navigating a building with many doors, we have to rely on signs and markers along the way to stay on track, moving towards the future God has for us. There may be detours or obstructions keeping us from going through certain doors, but if we are intentional, we will get where need to go.

Do we push through the obstacles or do we turn and run?

Your future is important to God. He has it all planned out, but He lets you partner in it. Don't think it's always a, "my way or the highway" mentality with God, because He is after a relationship with us. He wants us to journey with him.

> Ecclesiastes 3:11 (NIV): He has made everything beautiful in its time. He has also set eternity in the human heart: yet no one can fathom what God has done from beginning to end.

This verse tells us He knows everything but he has placed within us a sense of eternity, of our future, so that we can walk with Him. If we want to understand and experience some of His wonderful works, we should enjoy the present as we put our hope in Him for our future.

God opened the door of hope to each of us through Jesus. This is the first essential marker, or sign, that we follow along the route into the rest of our lives. After this, our journey becomes a partnership. We do our part, which is trust and obey, and He does His, which is guiding, keeping, loving, and growing us up in the Spirit. I don't know about you, but I'm going to pray and make sure I know which doors I should enter, or push open, or

Prayers that Make a Way

run away from.

Will we make mistakes? Probably; but not as many as if we were going through life alone.

*Lord, we are grateful that you have plans to prosper us and keep us safe, and plans that keep us hopeful about our future. (Jer. 29:11)*

*We are confident you who began a good work in us will carry it out until Jesus returns. (Phil. 1:6)*

*Thank you that you are the God of hope that fills us with all joy and peace as we trust in you. (Romans 15:13)*

*We will listen to your voice and accept discipline and at the end we will be counted wise.(Prov. 19:20-21)*

*We will trust in you with all our hearts and lean not on our own understanding; we acknowledge you and you will make our paths straight. (Prov. 3: 5-6)*

*Lord, it gives us much peace to know you are fully invested in our futures. You shed your blood and died for each one. Help us realize this truth more fully. Thank you for helping us find the doors that you are opening and give us wisdom to know when to walk through. In Jesus' name we pray. Amen.*

## ACKNOWLEDGMENTS

Most difficult things are not accomplished alone. That is why I would like to thank those that have supported me throughout this process.

I thank God for His voice—that He talks to me. Without His voice this book would not be.

My heart is full of gratitude to all my family and friends whom have always supported me and continued to do so throughout this new endeavor of becoming an author. God has blessed me abundantly with the most remarkable family and friends. I appreciate you all.

A special thank you to Jeffrey Pelton at Inscribe Press for making what could have been a very difficult process (editing/publishing) easy.

## ABOUT THE AUTHOR

Maria Aiello is a devoted wife, mother and educator who believes in the power of prayer. She has been writing on a personal level since high school, but most recently put her passion for prayer and writing together to comprise her first book. Maria serves on leadership at her local church and Aglow Lighthouse.

She lives in Pennsylvania with her husband, son, and beloved cat, Gary.

www.ingramcontent.com/pod-product-compliance
Lightning Source LLC
Chambersburg PA
CBHW021108080526
44587CB00010B/429